Getting into

Oxford &

Cambridge

2012 entry

Getting Into guides

Getting into Art & Design Courses, 7th edition
Getting into Business & Economics Courses, 9th edition
Getting into Dental School, 7th edition
Getting into Law, 8th edition
Getting into Medical School 2012 Entry, 16th edition
Getting into Physiotherapy Courses, 5th edition
Getting into Psychology Courses, 8th edition
Getting into US & Canadian Universities, 2nd edition
Getting into Veterinary School, 8th edition
How to Complete Your UCAS Application 2012 Entry, 23rd edition

Getting into

Oxford & Cambridge

2012 entry

Katy Blatt
14th edition

trotman | **t**

Getting into Oxford & Cambridge: 2012 Entry

This 14th edition published in 2011 by Trotman Publishing, an imprint of Crimson Publishing Limited, Westminster House, Kew Road, Richmond, Surrey TW9 2ND

© Trotman Publishing 2008, 2009, 2010, 2011

© Trotman & Co Ltd 1987, 1989, 1991, 1994, 1996, 1999, 2001, 2003, 2005, 2007

Author: Katy Blatt

13th edition by Katy Blatt
12th edition Sarah Alakija
11th edition by Natalie Lancer

Editions 7–10 by Sarah Alakija

British Library Cataloguing in Publication Data
A catalogue record for this book is available from the British Library.

ISBN: 978 1 84455 391 4

Typeset by IDSUK (Data Connection) Ltd.
Printed and bound in the UK by Ashford Colour Press, Gosport, Hants.

Contents

About the author   ix

Acknowledgements   xi

Foreword   xiii

Introduction: so you are thinking of applying to
Oxford or Cambridge   1

Why apply to Oxbridge?   3

1| Equal opportunities: am I eligible to apply?   7

Mature and young students   7
Students with disabilities and special educational
needs (SEN)   7
Students with children   8
Students from ethnic minorities   9
International students   10
Lesbian, gay, bisexual, and transsexual (LGBT)
students   11
Educationally disadvantaged students or students
who have had a disrupted education (and the
Cambridge Special Access Scheme)   11

2| Fees, financial support, and bursaries   13

The cost of studying at Oxbridge: changing tuition fees   13
Financial support and bursaries   15
Music awards and scholarships   16
Case study   17

3| The early stages of preparation   19

Choosing your A level subjects   19
Entry requirements   20

4| Choosing your course: the importance of reading   25

Why reading around your subject is essential
preparation for a good application   25
Recommended reading by subject   27

5| Experience to support your application   43

Gap years   43
Work experience   44
Case study   45

Contents

Events in your area 45
Case study 46

6| **Choosing your university and college** **49**

Choosing the university by subject 49
Differences in course structure at Oxford and Cambridge 50
Choosing the right college 51
Open applications 55

7| **UCAS and the Personal Statement** **57**

What qualities are the admissions tutors looking for? 57
A model Personal Statement 58
Extra-curricular experiences in the Personal Statement:
keeping everything relevant 60
Additional form for Cambridge: the Supplementary
Application Questionnaire (SAQ) 63
Submitting written work 65

8| **Written tests** **67**

BMAT (BioMedical Admissions Test), Oxford and
Cambridge 68
ELAT (English Literature Aptitude Test), Oxford only 70
HAT (History Aptitude Test), Oxford only 71
LNAT (The National Admissions Test for Law), Oxford only 74
Aptitude test for maths, Oxford only 75
Physics Aptitude Test, Oxford only 76
TSA (Thinking Skills Assessment), Oxford and Cambridge 78
STEP (Sixth Term Examination Papers), Cambridge only 79
Tests for modern languages, Oxford and Cambridge 82
Non-standardised tests at Cambridge (during interview) 83
General preparation for logic-based tests 83
Further reading 84

9| **The interview** **85**

Why are Oxford and Cambridge interviews important? 85
So what exactly are the interviewers looking for? 86
Interview styles 89
General preparation 92
Presentation skills: making an impression without words 104
The pooling system 105
Interview stories from previous applicants 106

10| **Getting the letter: offer or rejection and how to cope** **113**

A word on stress 114

Appendix 1: timetables **117**

The year before you apply 117
The year in which you apply 117

Appendix 2: glossary   **121**

Appendix 3: the UCAS form   **123**

Appendix 4: maps   **125**

Oxford map   125
Cambridge map   126

Postscript   **127**

About the author

After learning the violin with a teacher at the Royal College of Music in London, Katy Blatt studied art history at Cambridge University between 2003 and 2006. She graduated from the Courtauld Institute of Art in London in 2008 with an MA degree in 'Art and Cultural Politics in Germany, 1890–1945' after having co-curated the 'East Wing VIII – On Time' Exhibition (January 2008–July 2009) at Somerset House. She subsequently interned at the Museum of Modern Art in New York, where she helped research the 2009 Miró exhibition, and worked as the 'Schools and Teachers' intern at Tate Britain in their Youth Programmes Department. She has also worked as an educator at the Soane Museum in London (2007–2009). In March 2009 she began working at the MPW School, London, where she teaches art history and English language to 16–19 year olds.

Acknowledgements

Many thanks should go to all those who have previously written the Trotman guide to *Getting into Oxford & Cambridge*, particularly Sarah Alakija. Thanks also to those who have given subject-specific advice along the way, including John Meeske, Jim Burnett, Matthew Judd, Valeria Givone, Sarah Kemsley and Professor Mike Blatt.

Foreword

When I applied to Cambridge in 2001 I was 17 years old and pretty clueless. I wasn't really sure what I wanted to study at university. However, I did know, absolutely, that I wanted to go to Cambridge. I knew that what I loved more than anything in the world was to learn, to read, and to explore ideas; and I wanted to be somewhere that would foster these feelings. I knew about the special intellectual environment at Cambridge because I had been born there (whilst my father was completing his post-doctoral research) and I wanted a piece of it for myself.

I applied to read history at Clare College and, perhaps unsurprisingly, didn't get in. I was in the middle of my A levels and family upheavals, and I hadn't thought through my application. I loved history at school, but I hadn't done much extra reading. I hadn't formulated my own opinions and therefore I hadn't been able to express myself confidently at interview.

I was devastated when I received the letter of rejection: 'We are sorry to inform you that, upon careful consideration . . .' I sat on my bed in shock for about an hour and then pulled myself together. I looked at other universities, but there was nowhere else I wanted to go. I decided to take a gap year and to reapply to Cambridge having prepared more thoroughly.

When I went back to school the following day my art teacher suggested that I apply for a subject called art history – something that was not offered at my school. I read Gombrich's *The Story of Art* and had an immediate sense that this discipline would suit me perfectly. I loved art, I loved history, and I loved people. This was a subject that combined politics, sociology, history, psychology, and visual appreciation. What more could I ask for?

During my gap year I studied the violin at the Royal College of Music and practised for seven hours a day, every day. When I wasn't practising I read and read about art history. My boyfriend's father was an architect and I devoured every architectural history book on his shelves. I spent hours in the library, I went to every gallery and exhibition in every city I passed through, and I told everyone I met about what I was reading. I was determined that, by the time I went back to interview, I would know what I was talking about.

Towards the end of my gap year my grandmother suggested that I get some interview practice and directed me to the company Oxbridge

Applications, which offers mock interviews. I signed up and, with trepidation, attended several days of excellent interview practice. These mock interviews helped me overcome the anxiety I felt when talking to strangers about my subject and prepared me for the type of questions I might be asked at the real thing. When I was called to interview at Girton College, Cambridge in 2002 I set off with my four As at A level secured, a mature understanding of my chosen subject, and a confident attitude.

When I arrived at Girton for my interview I was relieved to find that, for every question I was asked, I had a considered answer to give. There were no strange questions or uncomfortable moments, just an interesting discussion which confirmed in my mind how much I wanted to learn more about this subject. The interviewers seemed to see this. I was in!

At Cambridge I met lots of intelligent and exciting young people: some of my best friends to this day. Most people who study there are ambitious and want to 'make a difference' in some way, and it was intensely satisfying as well as exhilarating to live in that environment. It was also incredibly exciting to have the freedom to explore. With only five hours of lectures a week and two hours of supervisions, I could organise my time as I wished. Most of my time was spent researching and writing essays but I managed to squeeze in time to lead the violin section in the university orchestra, sing in the college choir, attend my friends' philosophy lectures, and generally investigate other subjects.

Everyone applies to Oxbridge expecting to work harder than they have ever worked before. Sometimes I felt that my personal life was crushed under the sheer weight of expectation from supervisors and competition with peers. The level of stress was continuously high throughout the eight-week terms and during holidays there was always more reading and writing to do in preparation for the next term. Some people didn't cope well. The combination of living in a new environment away from home and the intensity of the work schedule meant that they became ill, depressed, or simply gave up. Half way through the first term I was seriously considering going back to music college. However, once I got into the swing of things the intellectual excitement of the place got to me like a drug that I didn't want to give up.

My three years at Cambridge were simultaneously gruelling, exhausting and wonderful. I read more, and faster, than I ever had before until sometimes I could practically feel my skull expanding. The quality of the academic support I was given (from my wonderful director of studies at King's, Jean Michel Massing) is, to this day, the best I have had in my life, and with this I found my intellectual confidence growing. The speed with which we were expected to produce essays was awesome (I had written four 2,500 word essays before my friends at other universities had written their first!) so, in order to cope, we all had to develop an ability to process and analyse information quickly. I emerged in the summer of 2006 as if out of some intellectual boot camp and feeling that I had had one of the most academically rigorous trainings in the world.

My arts degree at Cambridge did not prepare me for the 'world of work'. I have had to struggle with the transition from university to working life as much as any other recent graduate. The skills needed in graduate-level jobs are often not academic but practical, and an undergraduate degree in the arts from Cambridge is anything but practical. However, everyone knows – universities and employers – that the standard of Oxbridge graduates is very high. Oxbridge graduates are thought to be fast learners and speedy thinkers; people who are good at organising and communicating ideas. If we don't know how to do something at first employers can be sure that we will find out very swiftly. For this reason there is no doubt that a training at Oxford or Cambridge gains graduates positive recognition from employers and creates many opportunities that would not otherwise open up.

This book is intended to give bright young people some facts about the Oxbridge system and to demystify the application processes. There should not be secrets here, just hard work, dedication, and excitement about learning. I hope this book helps to create many more opportunities for talented students and I wish every reader luck in their quest for knowledge.

Katy Blatt, February 2011

Introduction
So you are thinking of applying to Oxford or Cambridge

If you are reading this book you are probably seriously thinking about applying to either Oxford University or Cambridge University. Good for you. It takes courage and guts to consider going for one of the most prestigious universities in the world. This fact puts many young people off. Oxbridge seems elusive to many potential applicants. They see the universities as magical, too expensive, and too brilliant for 'normal' people. These are misconceptions. At present, studying at Cambridge and Oxford is no more expensive than going to other universities (although this may change), and they are certainly not mythical places. They have a long history of excellence, but this should not put you off applying. What admissions tutors are looking for is students with real passion for their subject, enthusiasm to learn more, an ability to think critically and independently, and an outstanding academic track record. If you have these qualities don't be put off by the grandeur of Oxford and Cambridge: read on. This book aims to demystify the Oxbridge application process and to give you direction in your preparation for university.

It is worth noting here that this book will also be helpful to those students who do not end up applying or getting into Oxford or Cambridge. The university application process is complex and requires research and thought wherever you decide to study and this book is intended to help students approach these daunting choices. The equal opportunities section, the chapter on choosing a subject and university, and the section dedicated to writing your Personal Statement give useful advice for any UCAS application. Even if you do not end up needing to go for interview, having read the chapter about the interview process in this book will help build your self-esteem and give you tips on how to approach difficult academic situations, as well as giving insight into future job interviews.

Chapter 1, *Equal opportunities: am I eligible to apply*, aims to demystify the selection process by outlining Oxbridge's equal opportunities policy. It explains the policy for mature and young students; disabled students; students with children; students from ethnic minorities; international students; lesbian, gay, bisexual, and transsexual students; and educationally disadvantaged students or students who have had a disrupted education.

Chapter 2, *Fees, financial support, and bursaries*, explains the financial aspects of studying at Oxbridge. Many students are put off by the idea that studying at Oxbridge is more expensive than at other universities. This chapter explains that this is not the case, and gives a breakdown of costs incurred over one academic year. The chapter also introduces the bursary schemes at the universities, travel awards and music scholarships, and includes a case study of the spending habits of a new student at Cambridge.

Chapter 3, *The early stages of preparation*, discusses things you should consider well before the UCAS application. The chapter includes a section on choosing your A level subjects and the concept of 'soft' (unacceptable) A levels. It also discusses the importance of high grades and the alternatives to UK A levels that are accepted by Oxford and Cambridge (including the Baccalaureate and Scottish Highers).

Chapter 4, *Choosing your course: the importance of reading*, discusses the importance of choosing the right subject for you. Your choice of subject is more important than any other decision you will have to make during this process: more important than your choice of university and college. This chapter looks at the workload placed on students and the need to be prepared for this by reading widely and deeply. Also included in this section is a reading list to get you started.

Chapter 5, *Experience to support your application*, discusses the importance of extra-curricular experience in the application process. The issue of the 'gap year' is considered, and how this 'time out' can be advantageous in some circumstances but disadvantageous in others. It looks at the importance of work experience, particularly if you wish to study a vocational subject at university, and how it is essential to be aware of events in your area, current affairs, and news stories that are relevant to your chosen subject.

Chapter 6, *Choosing your university and college*, considers the best way to choose a university and college. It mentions the differences between Oxford and Cambridge, highlighting the importance of choosing the university that offers the subject that most suits you. Although this chapter includes the Tompkins and Norrington tables as points of reference, it advises against a tactical approach to college choice. Instead, it offers alternative methods for picking your future home. Finally, this chapter explains the option of the 'open application'.

Chapter 7, *UCAS and the Personal Statement*, gives advice about UCAS and the Personal Statement. Suggestions are given about how to make your application shine as well as example statements with analysis. After you have completed your Personal Statement, Cambridge (but not Oxford) automatically sends a Supplementary Application Questionnaire, and this chapter also gives advice on how to fill in this form. Many subjects require you to send in examples of written work, and this section explains why written work is required, for which subjects essay submissions are usual, and how best to satisfy the universities' requirements.

Chapter 8, *Written tests*, discusses the exams that are taken in addition to A levels as part of the application process for some subjects. These are taken either in advance of interviews or during the interview week in order to help interviewers decide on the best applicants. This chapter explains why these tests are necessary; gives lists of the subjects requiring additional testing at both Oxford and Cambridge; gives example questions, dates for testing and useful website links; as well as reading lists so that you can find out more for yourself.

Chapter 9, *The interview*, explains the interview process. General information about interview practice is given as well as a breakdown of what interviewers are looking for. In addition, there is information about different interview styles and how to deal with them; a comprehensive list of interview questions for a range of subjects; and six interview stories from previous applicants. Finally, there is a word of advice about presentation skills and an explanation of the pooling system.

Chapter 10, *Getting the letter: offer or rejection and how to cope*, looks at the final stages of the process: receiving an offer and coping with rejection; stress; and how you can make this experience a success, whether or not you obtain a place at Oxbridge.

In the appendices you will find: a useful timeline of the application process; a glossary of important words; a guide to completing the UCAS form; and, finally, maps of both Oxford and Cambridge with the locations of the colleges marked.

The remainder of this introduction explains why Oxford and Cambridge are worthwhile places to study, and why their tutorial, supervision and collegiate systems are still considered the best in the world.

Why apply to Oxbridge?

Oxford and Cambridge are the oldest universities in the United Kingdom. Founded in 1096 and in 1209 respectively by monastic orders, both universities have a wealth of history that pervades every courtyard. In both Oxford and Cambridge the universities form the hub of what were once medieval towns, and the students who live and work there are central to the vibrant life of both cities. Famous for their obscure traditions, you may have heard stories about undergraduates in dinner jackets at candlelit tables, extravagant drinking rituals, masked balls in the summer when the banks of the River Cam are lit by fireworks, and the secret societies whose members meet at midnight. This air of mystery is often propagated by the academics who work at Oxford and Cambridge perhaps because they enjoy the sense of authenticity and grandeur that this brings them. It is certainly true that, for hundreds of years, Oxford and Cambridge have attracted the most prestigious scholars in the world: Einstein and Stephen Hawking to name only two.

However, does this past grandeur and historical prestige translate into a world-class modern university education? Following are some of the reasons why Oxford and Cambridge are still two of the best educational institutions in the world and why they are worth applying to.

Perhaps one of the most distinctive features of an Oxbridge education, and one that is unique to these two institutions, is the tutorial/supervision system. Tutorials (at Oxford) and supervisions (at Cambridge) are hour-long weekly meetings that take place between one or two students and a member of the academic teaching staff at the students' college. These meetings are attended in addition to a related lecture series and are meant to add to students' knowledge of the subjects they are already studying. Essays and additional reading/problems to solve are set by the supervisor or tutor during the meetings as homework. The following week the marked work and/or reading set previously form the main topics of discussion.

This hour of academic mentoring offers intellectual nourishment that is generally unavailable at other universities. It is a rare privilege to get this degree of personal attention and intellectual support and students usually feel well cared for as well as learning a great deal from their teachers and peers. At these meetings students have the opportunity to discuss the strengths and weaknesses of their essays in detail, to ask questions about ideas they find interesting or confusing, and to learn to defend their arguments convincingly in person. This system also encourages students to develop their communication skills, to gain confidence when debating their ideas, and to listen to constructive criticism.

The collegiate system is also an integral part of the Oxbridge experience. Oxford and Cambridge are two very large universities (Oxford has about 11,500 undergraduate students and Cambridge about 10,500), but these vast institutions are made more cosy and personal through their division into colleges. Instead of applying to the university as a whole, prospective Oxbridge students normally apply to an individual college. Consisting of a food hall, where meals are prepared three times a day; bedrooms, which are cleaned daily; laundry rooms; and a bar, where students meet to unwind in the evenings, a student's college environment often forms the centre of his/her social life. Porters, stationed at the entrance to each college, watch the comings and goings of students, prevent the general public from intruding and generally keep a careful eye on the behaviour of 'freshers' (new students). Leaving home for the first time can be stressful and overwhelming so the social and pastoral network provided by the college creates a safe and comfortable environment in which to experience this transition.

The college also forms the hub of a student's academic life. Each undergraduate is assigned a 'director of studies' (DOS) at Cambridge or a 'tutor' at Oxford: a senior academic who is responsible for the intellectual development of their students. DOSs and tutors usually have their offices in the grounds of the college and can easily be called upon for help and advice. Although students sit exams with the rest of the university and can use university-wide resources (such as the university library) they benefit from the close contact of a small institution. Each college also has its own finances office, permanent staff and policies, and a surprising amount of autonomy and character.

There is no doubt that both Oxford and Cambridge offer a world-class education to this day. The calibre of academics and teaching staff at Oxford and Cambridge is equal to the best in the world and comparable to institutions such as Harvard and Yale in the United States. In 2011 the *Times Good University Guide* placed Oxford and Cambridge first and second respectively in the UK for teaching quality and student achievement. The 2011 the *Guardian University Guide* rankings also place Oxford and Cambridge in first and second place in the UK and, in the 2010 *Times Higher Education World University Rankings*, Cambridge was ranked first amongst world universities and Oxford was ranked seventh.

The list of distinguished people who have been educated at Oxbridge is huge: 40 prime ministers, including Tony Blair and David Cameron; at least 30 other international leaders including the present Archbishop of Canterbury and the Prime Minister of India; countless authors including Oscar Wilde, Philip Pullman, and J.R.R. Tolkien; the famous scientists Stephen Hawking, Richard Dawkins (author of *The God Delusion*), and Tim Berners-Lee (the co-inventor of the World Wide Web); the actors Hugh Grant and Michael Palin; and the filmmaker Ken Loach, all started their careers spending three years within the beautiful cloisters of Oxford and Cambridge. Not only is Oxbridge a hub of academic excellence and superb tutoring but it is also a nucleus of ideas, creative thinking, and networking.

I hope by now you will have been persuaded that Oxford and Cambridge are universities worth considering. If so, read on, and find out more about the application process and support available to you.

1 | Equal opportunities
Am I eligible to apply?

Cambridge and Oxford are two of the leading universities in the world, but this does not mean they are inaccessible. Their sole criterion for accepting new undergraduates is academic excellence. This is assessed through academic qualifications, during interviews, and through special written tests prior to interview. If you have good academic qualifications and are passionate about learning you are eligible and welcome to apply.

Mature and young students

Neither Cambridge nor Oxford specifies a minimum or maximum age at which students can apply, so all committed and academically capable students are welcome. However, some colleges may be wary of accepting you if you are 16 years old or younger at the time of application simply because they could be concerned that you may not be mature enough to cope with the university environment. You should telephone the admissions tutors at your chosen college if you are 16 or under to discuss this matter.

A mature student is defined as someone who is 21 years old by 1 October in the year in which they start their course. Mature students are attractive to both Cambridge and Oxford because they often display a more focused and serious attitude to their studies than their younger colleagues. If you are over 21, however, you may prefer to live in a college that admits a large number of mature students (Oxford has one and Cambridge has four of these colleges). The admissions process is the same for mature students as it is for non-mature applicants and the academic standard required is equally high for both. Naturally, work and life experience are taken into account when considering applications as well as previous academic qualifications. As with young students it is advisable to contact a college directly before making your application in order to discuss any concerns.

Students with disabilities and special educational needs (SEN)

Students with disabilities and SEN students are welcome at both universities and are in no way disadvantaged in their applications. Disabilities must be declared on the UCAS form in order for the university and college to pool their resources and you must contact the admissions office at university and college level to discuss your individual needs.

For students with physical disabilities and impaired movement, living in older colleges can be tricky. Because Oxford and Cambridge are so old much of the architecture is 'listed', meaning it is illegal to make substantial changes to the structure of the buildings. This means that it is sometimes impossible to install lifts. The same is true of some faculties, for example the architecture faculty at Cambridge. There are, however, many faculties with new buildings, which do not pose such problems, and several colleges in both universities have recently been renovated.

Students with dyslexia are given the opportunity to write using a computer and extra time during exams; they should feel in no way anxious about applying. Those with visual or hearing impairments are also welcome.

Each college should have a member of staff responsible for disabled students. You should ring the admissions tutor at your chosen college who will put you in touch with the disability staff member to discuss their resources and your needs. For more information see the links below.

- Cambridge Disability Resource Centre: www.admin.cam.ac.uk/univ/disability
- Oxford University Disability Advisory Service: www.admin.ox.ac.uk/eop/disab

Students with children

Both Oxford and Cambridge welcome applications from prospective students who have children. Several colleges provide accommodation for couples and families and some colleges have their own nurseries. There is also a university-wide nursery. You should ring the admissions office at your chosen college for more information.

The *Cambridge Guide for Student Parents* is written yearly by the Cambridge University Students' Union (CUSU) and is available online at: www.cusu.cam.ac.uk/welfare/childcare.

Some colleges are also members of the Central Childcare Bursary Scheme that makes means-tested grants available to overseas and EU students to help with the costs of childcare. Application forms are available from college offices, the Childcare Information Adviser, and CUSU. There are two rounds of applications with closing dates on 1 November and 1 March each year.

Oxford University provides similar support, heavily subsidising the cost of local nursery care, as well as funding holiday play schemes. See www.admin.ox.ac.uk/eop/child/students.shtml for further details.

Students from ethnic minorities

It must be said that the number of students from ethnic minorities at Oxbridge is low. This has generated a large amount of bad press both for Oxford and Cambridge, perhaps undeservedly. Statistics show that the percentage of minority applicants accepted out of those who apply is very similar to the percentage of white Western applicants who are successful. This suggests that the cause of under-representation of ethnic minorities is primarily the lack of applications from these groups rather than a bias against them, and both universities have outreach policies that aim to attract students from under-represented groups.

Cambridge University states in its Equal Opportunity Policy and Codes of Practice that:

> 'The University of Cambridge is committed in its pursuit of academic excellence to equality of opportunity and to a proactive and inclusive approach to equality, which supports and encourages all under-represented groups, promotes an inclusive culture, and values diversity. [The university promises to] monitor the recruitment and progress of all students . . . paying particular attention to the recruitment and progress of ethnic minority students and staff.'
>
> www.admin.cam.ac.uk/offices/hr/policy/equal.html

In its Race Equality Policy, Oxford University states that:

> 'The University of Oxford welcomes diversity amongst its students . . . recognising the contributions to the achievement of the University's mission that can be made by individuals from a wide range of backgrounds and experiences. The University aims to provide an inclusive environment which promotes equality, values diversity and maintains a working, learning and social environment in which the rights and dignity of all its . . . students are respected to assist them in reaching their full potential. The University will work to remove any barriers which might deter people of the highest potential and ability from applying to Oxford, either as staff or students.'
>
> www.admin.ox.ac.uk/eop/race/policy

Cambridge, in particular, is taking active steps to welcome students from ethnic minorities. The Group to Encourage Ethnic Minority Applications (GEEMA) was set up in 1989 to encourage applications from minority groups and to explain the application process to students who might otherwise not think of applying.

Email geema@cao.cam.ac.uk or Tel 01223 330873 for more information.

International students

International students are welcome at both Oxford and Cambridge and are valued members of the student population. International students make up less than 10% of the undergraduate population at Cambridge and 14% at Oxford. However, the percentages of overseas students increase at postgraduate level: at Cambridge 50% of postgraduates and at Oxford 63% of postgraduates are international students.

In order to study at Oxford and Cambridge your **English** must be of a high standard. This is measured by your performance in various different examinations including:

- the IELTS (International English Language Testing System) in which you need a score of at least 7.0 in each section (speaking, listening, writing, and reading)
- the English Language GCSE examination at grade B (for Oxford) or C (for Cambridge)
- the TOEFL (Test of English as a Foreign Language) exam, scoring at least 100
- for EU students, a high grade in English taken as part of a leaving examination (for example the European Baccalaureate and the Abitur) may be acceptable
- an A grade in the Cambridge Certificate in Advanced English or the Cambridge Certificate of Proficiency in English.

The level of English proficiency required depends a great deal on which subject you wish to study. If you want to apply for an essay-based subject (any of the arts or social science subjects including economics, PPE, psychology, history, and English literature) your written work must be fluent. On the other hand English language is much less important for the study of mathematics.

> For information about the IELTS exam and where and when it can be taken, visit: www.ielts.org.

The **cost** of studying at a UK university for an international student is much higher than for a home student. The tuition fees at Cambridge for the academic year 2009–10 range from £9,747 to £12,768 for most courses although clinical medicine costs £23,631. At Oxford fees range from £11,750 to £13,450 and for clinical medicine you are asked to pay £24,500. For more information go to the following websites.

Cambridge:

- international students: www.cam.ac.uk/admissions/undergraduate/international/

- financial issues for international students: www.cam.ac.uk/admissions/undergraduate/international/scholarships.html
- electronic application form: www.cam.ac.uk/admissions/undergraduate/apply/forms/coaf.pdf

Oxford:

- International Students Information and Advisory Service: www.admin.ox.ac.uk/io
- official site, including entrance requirements, international qualifications etc.: www.ox.ac.uk/admissions/undergraduate_courses/international_students/information_for_international_applicants
- fees for international students: www.admin.ox.ac.uk/studentfunding/fees
- international student application forms from: www.admissions.ox.ac.uk/forms

Lesbian, gay, bisexual, and transsexual (LGBT) students

Oxford and Cambridge are pluralist universities. Not only is there a central LGBT society at each university but each college also has its own LGBT representative. There are plenty of events to help you feel comfortable. For further information go to these websites.

- Cambridge LesBiGay information from CUSU: www.lgbt.cusu.cam.ac.uk
- Oxford LesBiGay at OUSU: www.ousu.org/about/campaigns/a/lgbtq

Educationally disadvantaged students or students who have had a disrupted education (and the Cambridge Special Access Scheme)

Oxford and Cambridge are committed to helping applicants who have in some way been disadvantaged by a poor school education or by significant disruption to their educational career, which may have resulted in candidates getting lower grades at A level than they might otherwise have achieved.

Cambridge University, in particular, caters for these students with its Cambridge Special Access Scheme (CSAS). On its website, Cambridge states that:

'Admissions Tutors are aware that some applicants may not be predicted the high grades required, but will nevertheless have

> *the potential and motivation to follow a course at Cambridge*
> *successfully. CSAS . . . is designed to ensure that Colleges*
> *have the information they require in order to accurately assess*
> *applicants who have experienced particular social or educational*
> *disadvantage.'*
>
> *www.sel.cam.ac.uk/prospectus/home/index.php?m=file&f=72*

The CSAS is open to UK and EU students only and applicants will be considered if either:

- few people from the applicant's school/college proceed to higher education and the applicant's family has little or no tradition of entry to higher education to study for a degree; or
- the applicant's education has been significantly disrupted or disadvantaged through health or personal problems, disability, or difficulties with schooling.

Schools/colleges must complete a CSAS form on behalf of the student in question as individual applications are not considered. For more information, go to: www.sel.cam.ac.uk/prospectus/home/index.php?m=file&f=72.

2 | Fees, financial support, and bursaries

The cost of studying at Oxbridge: changing tuition fees

The coalition government has recently announced that the cost of tuition fees will be allowed to rise for those starting university in 2012. Although final decisions have not yet been published, it has been said that Oxford and Cambridge are likely to charge around £9,000. You may well be anxious about the extent of this rise in fees, however do not let it put you off applying. As in previous years tuition fees can be covered by the government through student loans, which do not have to be repaid until you are earning £20,000 per year or above. In addition, the Office of Fair Access has stated that universities that intend to charge these high tuition fees must first prove that they plan to implement more proactive and far-reaching access schemes than they are running currently. Living costs at Oxbridge are subsidised, so the cost of accommodation and food is as cheap, if not cheaper, than at other universities, whilst there has long been a tradition of bursaries and additional support for exceptionally talented students who would otherwise not be able to afford a place. In addition there will be a new £150m government-funded National Scholarship Programme to help students from lower income families.

Decisions concerning tuition fees may not be finalised until mid-2011, so you should keep a close eye on the Cambridge and Oxford fees and funding websites. For more information and updates go to the web pages below.

- Cambridge: http://www.cam.ac.uk/admissions/undergraduate/finance/2012entry
- Oxford: http://www.ox.ac.uk/feesandfunding/fees
- Directgov (for forthcoming fees as well as financial support and bursaries): http://www.direct.gov.uk/en/EducationAndLearning/UniversityAndHigherEducation/StudentFinance/DG_194804

Living expenses

Room rental at both universities is normally between £70 and £100 per week and students do not have to pay rent during holidays if they go home. Room rental also includes the cost of electricity and hot water so students do not need to be concerned about additional costs.

You may choose to buy your own food and cook for yourself and, if so, the amount you spend will largely depend on your tastes and shopping habits. It is possible to live on a shoestring.

There is usually a small, obligatory charge for the use of a college kitchen (between £12 and £15 per week). This is payable whether or not you cook regularly.

Alternatively there are three meals each day provided by every college's food 'halls' and these are subsidised: generally a three-course meal will cost no more than £3. At most colleges the kitchen staff take Sunday nights off, leaving students to fend for themselves. So, for at least one night, you will either need to cook in your corridor's kitchen or eat out.

Clothes-washing is done in the laundry room and tokens can be purchased from the porter's lodge at approximately £1.20 per load.

Transport

Getting around in Cambridge and Oxford is very cheap, if not free. If it is raining some students prefer to take the bus to their lectures at a cost of about £1 per ride. However, most students cycle everywhere. This is by far the fastest and the cheapest way to travel. If you don't have a bike already you can pick one up from one of the many second-hand bike shops in both cities from as little as £35 (although if you want a better ride you will obviously have to pay more). Additional costs to consider when investing in a bike include: the helmet at approximately £25; locking systems to prevent theft (very important) at about £15–20; and servicing charges. There are many bike mechanics across both cities who will fix your bike for a fee. However, college porters usually have free bike repair kits and there are normally bike 'reps' at each college: students who you can call on for help mending and servicing your wheels for absolutely no charge.

Study materials

The amount you will need to spend on study materials depends upon which subject you wish to take. For example, scientists may need to purchase lab coats and mathematicians may need to buy calculators. You may be tempted to buy the books on your pre-course reading list. By all means purchase books if your faculty recommend you do this. However, remember that all these books will certainly be held in the university library, the faculty library, and even in your college library. So you needn't spend much.

Overall, your spending per year might look like this:

- tuition fees: £3,290 (open to change)
- living costs: £6,000–£7,500 per year (including accommodation: £70–£100/week, kitchen charges of £12–£15 per week)
- college meals: £2–£3 per meal
- transport: £150 per year (including bike servicing).

Financial support and bursaries

Financial support is available for students who might find it difficult to afford to go to university. Both universities make it very clear that they are primarily interested in students' academic abilities and not their socio-economic background.

As the Oxford prospectus explains:

> 'If you can get in, we can help out . . . At Oxford your mind is the only asset we're interested in.'
>
> *Oxford Prospectus, 2009*

On the Cambridge University website it describes the Cambridge Bursary Scheme:

> 'We are committed to the principle that no UK student should be deterred from applying to the University of Cambridge because of financial concerns, and that no student should have to leave because of financial difficulties. As a result we have one of the most extensive financial support programmes in the UK to ensure that students can meet the cost of the Cambridge education, regardless of background.'
>
> *Cambridge Prospectus, Guide for Parents and Supporters, 2009 (www.cam.ac.uk/admissions/ undergraduate/publications/parentsguide.pdf)*

Bursaries at both universities are worth approximately £12,000–£14,000 and these are made available to students in financial distress. In addition, most of the colleges have large endowments and can provide their own bursaries, grants, and scholarships to students who are in need or who are exceptionally academically gifted. Financial rewards are given to students who achieve highly in exams, and most colleges will provide funding for travel in the summer holidays if the excursion is relevant to your studies.

Although both universities have an umbrella policy for supporting students financially, each college has different resources at its disposal. Therefore, you need to ring the admissions tutor at each college separately to ask their advice on the issue. For more information follow the links below.

Cambridge:

- bursaries and financial support: www.newtontrust.cam.ac.uk/world/cbs/2009/funding
- financial information: www.cam.ac.uk/admissions/undergraduate/finance/support.html

Oxford:

- bursaries and financial support: www.ox.ac.uk/admissions/undergraduate_courses/student_funding
- financial information: www.ox.ac.uk/feesandfunding

Music awards and scholarships

These are awarded to exceptionally talented musicians. Both Oxford and Cambridge are renowned for the high quality of music that they foster. Each college has a chapel which holds daily or weekly services and most colleges have two organ scholars and a choir. Singers must be of semi-professional standard and dedicate up to six hours a week to rehearsals. Both organ scholarships and choral scholarships are very competitive but are worth up to several thousand pounds a year depending on which college you apply to.

At Cambridge each college gives annual instrumental awards amounting to several hundred pounds per year as well as a chamber music scheme where students are trained by the university's resident quartet and are awarded an annual stipend. The size of the stipend depends upon the college's wealth and funding priorities.

At Oxford, in addition to choral scholarships, there are répétiteur (musical theatre) scholarships.

The application deadline for these awards is in September of the year before you are due to start at university (a month before the UCAS deadline for Oxbridge). For more information follow the links below.

Cambridge:

- for choral and organ scholarships go to: www.cam.ac.uk/admissions/undergraduate/musicawards/choral.html
- for instrumental awards: www.cam.ac.uk/admissions/undergraduate/musicawards

Oxford:

- download a leaflet for organ, choral, and répétiteur scholarships at: www.music.ox.ac.uk/admissions/organ-and-choral-scholarships1/Organandchoralscholarships-main-page.html

Case study: Nancy Parker, first year student at Cambridge in October 2009

I started my first year at Cambridge in October 2009. It was pretty daunting at first, managing my finances for the first time on my own. Cambridge is so grand and I was really afraid that I would spend a huge amount of money in the first term and then be completely skint for the rest of the year. However, the cost of living and working at Cambridge was less than I expected, and there were perks.

When I arrived I wanted to know whether I would have to pay for electricity, water, and gas separately since, obviously, that's how my parents pay for bills at home. However, at college, bills for heating and water etc. are all included in the room/accommodation charge. I had a small but cosy room this year and I paid £70 per week for it. I also had to pay a small charge of £50 per term for using the kitchen on my corridor. Both these costs were covered by my student loan. What is really helpful is that I didn't have to pay for accommodation during the holidays. That means I only paid for 24–30 weeks this year. It's helpful for us students and good for the college too since they can rent the rooms out for conferences during the holidays.

In terms of food, I do a relatively big shop at the start of each week. I take my bike basket and a big backpack and stuff as much in as I can. I generally get bread and fresh fruit for lunches and cereal for breakfast. I also get things like tea bags, milk and chocolate to keep me going during the weekly essay crisis! That all comes to about £15 per week. Then I eat my evening meals in halls with my friends, which comes to about £15 per week too. So, overall, I tend not to spend more than £30 per week on food.

Travel for me is completely – or almost completely – free. I have a bike which I took up from home, and I go everywhere with it: to lectures, food shops, to meet friends. I have a rainproof coat and trousers which I wear when the weather is bad, and I continue to cycle even then. Alternatively I walk to lectures, which takes about 20 minutes because I live on the other side of town from my faculty. I reckon I spent about £100 over the whole year on bike repairs, so not too much at all. I did also have to invest in an extra strong bike lock, which cost £30. It was worth it though because my bike is still with me after a year when some of my friends used flimsy locks and had their bikes nicked.

The only other thing I have spent money on this year is going out. I don't really go out that often, perhaps once a week. To be honest there isn't enough time in the day, what with the amount of work piled on us. My evening often consists of meeting up in one of my friends' rooms and having a tea and a chat or going to the college bar to chill. I reckon I spent about £10–£20 per week last term on going out. However, everyone's different. Loads of students I know go out much more. It really depends how much you like to drink and how often you want to party. Of course there are things like clothes and shoes to buy but those, again, are not necessities.

There have also been times when the college has paid *me*. For example, this year I really wanted to visit Venice since I was studying the culture of the city in a module of my course. I applied for a travel grant from my college and they gave me £300 towards the cost of my trip.

Also, I am a serious flute player and I applied for a bursary towards the cost of my lessons. I had an audition and I won an instrumental award. The college paid me £150 per term on the condition that I played in the end of term concert. I am going to go for it again next year.

There's also a bursary scheme that's really helpful. My parents can't afford to help me out, so I get the full amount of over £3,000 per year, and loads of people I know either get the same or at least some financial contribution from their college. There is also something called a hardship fund. This means that if something goes drastically wrong, the college can bail you out. Of course they would only do this if you had a real need and not if you had overspent at Top Shop.

Budgeting is really important, and it's really important to spend carefully. But, if you keep track of your money and make the most of the support on offer from your university and college, it is definitely possible to live comfortably here.

3| The early stages of preparation

Choosing your A level subjects

Usually, if you want to study at Oxford or Cambridge, admissions tutors will expect you to have studied your chosen subject at AS and A level and to have got a high A grade (at least 90%). This is true of mainstream subjects, such as English, history and mathematics. However, there are some subjects taught at Cambridge and Oxford that do not require you to have taken a previous qualification in the subject.

Subjects that do not require a specific A level include:

- Anglo-Saxon, Norse, and Celtic
- archaeology and anthropology
- classical archaeology and ancient history
- classics (Cambridge)
- geography (Cambridge – at Oxford they do want Geography A level)
- history of art
- human sciences
- land economy (Cambridge)
- law
- oriental sciences
- philosophy (Cambridge)
- philosophy and theology
- philosophy, politics and economics (PPE; Oxford)
- social and political science (SPS; Cambridge)
- theology.

It is also important to bear in mind that some subjects that are available at A level are not rated highly by Oxford and Cambridge. This is because they feel these subjects do not prepare students for the kind of analytical and problem-solving work expected in higher education. Cambridge even has a list on its website of unacceptable or 'soft' A level subjects that it will not accept.

Cambridge's list of 'soft' A levels includes:

- accounting
- art and design (this may be acceptable in some cases; for example, for fine art at Oxford it is acceptable. Architecture departments may also accept this subject)

- business studies
- communication studies
- dance
- design and technology (this may be acceptable in some cases – check engineering requirements)
- drama/theatre studies (this may be acceptable in some cases – check education and English requirements, for Cambridge only)
- film studies
- general studies (as a fourth A level only)
- health and social care
- home economics
- information and communication technology
- leisure studies
- media studies
- music technology
- performance studies
- performing arts
- photography
- physical education
- sports studies
- travel and tourism
- world development.

If you do want to take, or have already taken, one of the above subjects, this is not the end of the world. However, make sure you have taken at least three 'hard' subjects that are relevant to your chosen course in addition to a fourth 'soft' subject. In some cases 'soft' subjects may even complement your application. If you wish to study English litera-ture, for example, it could be helpful to study theatre studies as this subject will give you insight into the performative aspects of writing for the stage.

Entry requirements

Many students apply to Oxford and Cambridge every year on the strength of the universities' reputation. However, because their fame extends across continents, both universities can afford to be choosy about who they invite to interview. When inviting prospective students to interview, the first thing admissions tutors look at is your exam results. Although the Oxbridge prospectuses generally talk in terms of English qualifications it should be noted that other school and national examina-tions equivalent to English A levels and GCSEs are equally acceptable. The text below gives details of the qualifications acceptable to Oxford and Cambridge and the grades that are expected of you at both institu-tions. For more detailed information about entrance requirements see the following websites.

- Cambridge: www.cam.ac.uk/admissions/undergraduate/apply/ requirements.html#course
- Oxford: www.admissions.ox.ac.uk/int/quals

Cambridge Special Access Scheme

If you feel you will not achieve the grades you are capable of, whether for health reasons or because your school has not given you the support you need, and you are a student from the UK and EU, may apply, via your school, for the Cambridge Special Access Scheme (see Chapter 1).

A levels

If you are taking your exams in England you should aim to achieve three or four A grades at AS and A level. You should bear in mind that most students who apply will have, or be predicted, these grades. Universities are now able to see the breakdown of your marks for each subject and it is expected that you get 100% in at least one module in the subject you wish to continue studying at university.

Whereas Oxford will not be using the new A* grade at A level in its offers for 2012, Cambridge welcomes their introduction. An A* will be awarded to students who achieve an A grade overall at A level and also achieve an average of 90% or more on the uniform mark scale (UMS) across their A2 units. The standard A level conditional offer made by the Cambridge colleges for 2012 entry will be A*AA. The subject in which the A* is to be achieved is unlikely to be specified in most cases although it makes sense to achieve the A* in the subject you wish to continue studying at university.

GCSEs

Admissions tutors will also look closely at your GCSE grades. A good applicant will typically have taken 10 or more GCSEs and obtained A and A* grades in all of them.

International Baccalaureate Diploma Programme

Offers are regularly made on the International Baccalaureate at A level of between 7, 6, 6 and 7, 7, 7 in the Higher level subjects, with overall scores between 38 and 42 points out of 45.

Scottish Highers and Advanced Highers

Oxbridge welcome applicants with Scottish qualifications. They do not normally make offers on the basis of Highers alone and will normally expect applicants to have achieved a minimum of four A grades at Higher grade plus Advanced Highers. Offers will usually be AAB or AAA in three Advanced Highers. In some cases two Advanced Highers and an additional Higher may be acceptable.

Welsh Baccalaureate

Oxbridge welcome applications from students taking the Advanced Diploma in the Welsh Baccalaureate. Applicants will be expected to have studied three subjects at A level as part of their qualification. Offers will be conditional on achievement in the A levels within the qualification rather than the overall Baccalaureate award.

Irish Leaving Certificate

Applicants from the Republic of Ireland who are studying towards the Irish Leaving Certificate are also welcome to apply. Typical offers for the Irish Leaving Certificate vary from AAAAA to AAABB at Higher level.

Access to HE Diploma

If you are considering applying to Oxbridge as a mature student and are studying for an Access to HE Diploma, the universities require 60 credits with a minimum of 45 credits at level 3 (or equivalent). Applicants may be required to meet additional subject-specific requirements for particular courses at Cambridge. Details of these additional requirements are listed at: www.cam.ac.uk/admissions/undergraduate/apply/requirements.html#alevel. For further information you may contact the FE Access Officer in the Cambridge Admissions Office (Email feaccess@cao.cam.ac.uk Tel 01223 765728) or the admissions staff in one of the Cambridge colleges.

European Baccalaureate

If you are studying towards the European Baccalaureate, note that successful applicants are typically asked for 85% overall with 90% in those subjects that relate most closely to the course they wish to study.

French Baccalaureate

Typical offers for applicants taking the French Baccalaureate are 16 or 17 ('mention très bien') out of 20. Applicants are also usually asked to achieve 16 or 17 in specific subjects.

German Abitur

If you are studying towards the German Abitur, note that applicants are typically asked for an overall score of between 1.0 and 1.3, with 13 or 14 in those subjects that relate most closely to the course they wish to study.

Cambridge Pre-U

Cambridge Pre-U is a post-16 qualification designed to prepare students with the skills important at university. It challenges students to show not only a keen grasp of their subject, but also lateral, critical, and contextual thinking. It encourages independent research and promotes learning through innovative approaches to the curriculum and assessment. Both universities will accept the Pre-U but express no preference for it over any other qualification.

The Extended Project

The Extended Project is a separate qualification that A level students may add to their study programme. Students carry out a project on a topic of their choosing which may or may not be linked to their chosen A level subjects. The projects involve planning, research, and evaluation, but the end product may be in the form of a dissertation, a performance, or an artefact. The aim of the Extended Project is to develop research and independent learning skills that will be of great benefit in higher education and employment. Currently neither university uses the Extended Project in its offers, but they both recognise the benefits: the skills which can ease the transition from secondary to higher education.

Cambridge has stated that the Extended Project may be a suitable topic for discussion at interview and in some cases, where it is relevant, it may be an appropriate piece of written work to be submitted.

The Diploma

The specialised Diploma for 14–19 year olds has been created to provide an alternative to more traditional qualifications. Both Oxford and Cambridge will accept the Advanced Diploma in Engineering for applicants to their engineering courses. However, applicants for engineering will also need A level Physics and the level 3 Certificate in Mathematics. Neither university has made any statement about their acceptance of other Diploma subjects.

4| Choosing your course
The importance of reading

Why reading around your subject is essential preparation for a good application

Choosing the right course is the most important decision you will have to make during the whole application process. It is primarily your enthusiasm for your subject that will be attractive to the admissions tutors and interviewers and, if you are accepted, your love for your subject will sustain you through hours of hard work. When considering which course to take and then preparing for interview, reading is another, and absolutely essential, form of preparation. You need to read widely and deeply. Knowing the school syllabus is not enough. You need to be able to think and talk about ideas beyond the scope of school work and above the level of your peers.

Remember that the academics who teach at Oxford and Cambridge, and who interview prospective students, have dedicated their whole lives to their subject. They believe passionately in the importance of their research and expect you to do the same. If you have read around your subject this shows that you are dedicated and passionate and this will be very attractive to interviewers.

In addition, if you get accepted, the vast majority of your time as an undergraduate will be spent working. There is probably more responsibility and expectation placed on students at Oxbridge than at any other university in the UK. Reading around your subject will prepare you for the work you are about to undertake. Good students at Oxford and Cambridge will typically work for 10 hours per day – sometimes more during exam term. Whereas students on an essay-based course at UCL, for example, will be asked to write four 2,500-word essays over the course of a 10-week term, Oxbridge students are asked to write between 12 and 14 essays of the same length in the course of an eight-week term. Students who study science subjects at Oxbridge will have a vast amount of contact time per week. These hours are made up of lab sessions, supervisions, seminars, and lectures that fill up most of the day, every day of the working week. There is little time off, and most of it is taken up studying for assignments and short essays. The more excited you are by this work, the more likely your experience will be tolerable and worthwhile.

Reading widely and deeply is also an essential preparation for the style of working you will be expected to do at university. The method of working at Oxbridge is very different from school. Students who study humanities subjects (English literature, history, and languages, for example) typically have very few hours of contact time in the week; perhaps six to eight hours of lectures and one hour-long seminar per week. However, they are expected to work as many hours as the scientists. This requires them to be incredibly independent in their study practice. Humanities students need to be dedicated, focused, and able to follow through their own research without getting distracted. Like the scientists, therefore, humanities students need to show they are able to research independently in preparation for the interview.

Finally, in order to make the right choice it is important to gather as much information about a course and its content as possible. Prospectuses for Oxford and Cambridge give detailed course guides, including information on course content and A level requirements. In addition, Oxford makes individual prospectuses for each subject. Read this information and the criteria very carefully, making sure your qualifications fulfil the requirements specified.

If you want to be really thorough, contact the individual faculty secretaries at the university. Remember that, while the college administers the teaching, it is the faculty (i.e. the subject department within the university) that controls the syllabus. The faculty secretary will have much more detail on course content than is available in the prospectuses. Information about faculty addresses, including website addresses, is available in the prospectuses; Cambridge applicants may also refer to *The Cambridge University Guide to Courses*, published by Cambridge University Press.

When you talk with the faculty secretary ask him or her for an up-to-date reading list for new undergraduates. This will list the books that students are expected to read before they come up to Cambridge or Oxford for the first time. If you dip into some of these books you will get an idea of the sort of information you will be tackling if you study the subject. In addition, if you have time to visit Cambridge or Oxford again, you could spend the afternoon in the university bookshop (Blackwell's in Oxford or Heffers in Cambridge). The staff at both bookshops are very familiar with the texts used by undergraduates. Of course, if you know any current undergraduates at either university, discuss their work with them.

Collecting this information will boost your confidence and reassure you about your subject decision. Remember, in order to argue your case at interview, and to cope with the workload if you get a place, you must be deeply committed to your subject.

Recommended reading by subject

The following is a list of suggested books and films that may help you to start your research. This list is not exhaustive or essential reading but it will give you some direction. Don't feel you must read every book on this list, either. Dip into one or two to start with and see what particularly interests you. If your subject is not included here, or if you want to find out more, go to the faculty or college website to get a longer list.

Archaeology and anthropology

Social anthropology

- Fox, K., *Watching the English*. London: Hodder & Stoughton, 2007.
- Monaghan, J. and Just, P., *Social and Cultural Anthropology: A Very Short Introduction*. Oxford: OUP, 2000.

Biological anthropology

- Clack, T., *Ancestral Roots: Modern Living and Human Evolution*. Basingstoke: Palgrave Macmillan, 2008.
- Lewin, R., *Human Evolution: An Illustrated Introduction*. Oxford: Blackwell, 2005.

Archaeology

- Gamble, C., *Archaeology: The Basics*. Abingdon: Routledge, 2000.
- Renfrew, C. and Bahn, P., *Archaeology: Theories, Methods and Practice*. London: Thames & Hudson, 2008.

General books

- Barley, N., *The Innocent Anthropologist: Notes From A Mud Hut*. Long Grove, IL: Waveland, 2000.
- Carrithers, M., *Why Human Beings Have Cultures*. Oxford: OUP, 1992.
- Dunbar, R., *Gossip, Grooming and the Evolution of Language*. London: Faber, 1996.
- Fagan, B., *People of the Earth: An Introduction to World Prehistory*. London: Longman, 2004.
- Gosden, C., *Anthropology and Archaeology: A Changing Relationship*. Abingdon: Routledge, 1999.
- Harrison, G. A., *Human Biology: An Introduction to Human Evolution, Variation, Growth, and Adaptability*. Oxford: OUP, 1992.

- Haviland, W., *Cultural Anthropology*. London: Harcourt Brace, 2003.
- Hendry, J., *An Introduction to Social Anthropology: Other People's Worlds*. London: Macmillan, 1999.
- Keesing, R. and Strathern, A., *Cultural Anthropology: A Contemporary Perspective*. London: Harcourt Brace, 1998.
- Kuper, A., *The Chosen Primate: Human Nature and Cultural Diversity*. Cambridge, MA: Harvard University Press, 1996.
- Layton, R., *An Introduction to Anthropological Theory*. Cambridge: CUP, 1997.

Architecture

Also look at the reading list for art history.

- Kenneth Frampton, *Modern Architecture, A Critical History*.
- Le Corbusier, *Towards a new Architecture*.
- Steen Eiler Rasmussen, *Experiencing Architecture*.
- John Summerson, *The Classical Language of Architecture*.
- Vitruvius, *The Ten Books on Architecture*.
- David Watkin, *The History of Western Architecture*.

Art history

- H.H. Arnason and Peter Kalb, *History of Modern Art*, 5th edition, 2002.
- Michael Baxandall, *Painting and Experience in Fifteenth Century Italy: A Primer in the Social History of Pictorial Style*, 1972 and later edns.
- Mary Beard and John Henderson, *Classical Art From Greece to Rome*, 2001.
- John Berger, *Ways of Seeing*, 1972.
- John Boardman, ed., *Oxford History of Classical Art*, 1993.
- Michael Camille, *Gothic Art: Glorious Visions*, 1996.
- Craig Clunas, *Art in China*, 2nd edition, 2009.
- Thomas Crow, *The Rise of the Sixties: American and European Art in the Era of Dissent*, 1996.
- Jas Elsner, *Imperial Art and Christian Triumph: The Art of the Roman Empire, 100–450*, 1998.
- E.H. Gombrich, *The Story of Art*, 1950 and later edns.
- Michael Greenhalgh, *The Classical Tradition in Art*, 1978.
- Craig Harbison, *The Mirror of the Artist: Northern Renaissance Art in its Historical Context*, 1995.
- Francis Haskell, *History and Its Images: Art and the Interpretation of the Past*, 1993.
- Hugh Honour and John Fleming, *A World History of Art*, 7th edition, 2005.

- Geraldine A. Johnson, *Renaissance Art: A Very Short Introduction*, 2002.
- Linda Nochlin, *Women, Art and Power and other essays*, 1989.
- J.J. Pollitt, *Art and Experience in Classical Greece*, 1972.
- Vasari, *Lives of* the *Artists*, first published 1555.
- David Watkin, *A History of Western Architecture*.
- Mariët Westermann, *A Worldly Art: The Dutch Republic 1585–1718*, 1996.

Biological sciences (Oxford)

- Burton, R., *Biology by Numbers: An Encouragement to Quantitative Thinking*. Cambridge: CUP, 1998.
- Chalmers, A.F., *What is This Thing Called Science?* Maidenhead: Open University Press, 1998.
- Collins, H.M. and Pinch, T., *The Golem: What You Should Know About Science*, 2nd edition. Cambridge: CUP, 1998.
- Coyne, J., *Why Evolution is True*. Oxford: OUP, 2009.
- Freedman, D., Pisani, R. and Purves, R., *Statistics*, 3rd edition (although any edition would do). New York: W.W. Norton and Company Ltd., 1997.
- Southwood, R., *The Story of Life*. Oxford: OUP, 2003.

Biochemistry (Oxford)

- Alberts *et al.*, *Molecular Biology of the Cell*, 5th edition. Abingdon: Taylor & Francis, 2008.
- Alberts *et al.*, *Essential Cell Biology*, 2nd edition. Abingdon: Taylor & Francis, 2003.
- Campbell and Farrell, *Biochemistry*, 6th edition. Andover: Cengage Learning, 2008.
- Devlin, *Textbook of Biochemistry with Clinical Correlation*, 6th edition. Chichester: Wiley-Liss, 2005.
- Elliott and Elliott, *Biochemistry and Molecular Biology*, 3rd edition. Oxford: OUP, 2004.
- Fox and Whitesell, *Organic Chemistry*, 3rd edition. Sudbury, MA: Jones & Bartlett, 2004.
- Garret and Grisham, *Biochemistry*, 3rd edition. Andover: Cengage Learning, 2005.
- Lewin, Cassimeris, Lingappa, and Plopper (eds), *Cells*, 1st edition. Sudbury, MA: Jones & Bartlett, 2007.
- Lodish et al, *Molecular Cell Biology*, 6th edition. New York, NY: W.H. Freeman, 2008.
- Stryer *et al.*, *Biochemistry*, 6th edition. New York, NY: W.H. Freeman, 2004.
- Sykes, *Guidebook to Mechanism in Organic Chemistry*, 6th edition. Englewood Cliffs, NJ: Prentice Hall, 1986.

- Voet, D., Voet J. and Pratt, C., *Fundamentals of Biochemistry*, 3rd edition. Chichester: John Wiley & Sons, 2008.

Economics

- Dasgupta, P., *Economics: A Very Short Introduction*.
- Jacques, I., *Mathematics for Economics and Business*.
- *The Economist* (weekly).
- *Financial Times*.

Microeconomics

- Begg, D.K.H., Fischer, S. and Dornbusch, R., *Economics* (latest edition). Maidenhead: McGraw-Hill, 2005.
- Dixit, A. and Skeath, S., *Games of Strategy* (2nd edition). New York, NY: Norton, 2009.
- Morgan, W., Katz, M. and Rosen, S., *Microeconomics* (latest edition). Maidenhead: McGraw-Hill, 2005.
- Varian, H., *Intermediate Microeconomics* (latest edition). New York, NY: Norton, 2010.

Macroeconomics

- Heilbroner, R., *The Worldly Philosophers* (latest edition). London: Penguin, 2000.
- Mankiw, N.G. and Taylor, M.P., *Macroeconomics* (European edition). New York, NY: W.H. Freeman, 2007.

Quantitative methods in economics

- Aczel, A.D., and Sounderpandian, J., *Complete Business Statistics* (latest edition). Maidenhead: McGraw-Hill/Irwin, 2008.
- Bradley, T. and Patton, P., *Essential Mathematics for Economics and Business* (latest edition). Chichester: Wiley, 2008.
- Lind, D., Marchal W. and Mason, R., *Statistical Techniques in Business and Economics* (latest edition). Maidenhead: McGraw-Hill/Irwin, 2009.
- Pemberton, M. and Rau, N., *Mathematics for Economists* (2nd edition). Manchester: Manchester University Press, 2006.

Political and sociological aspects of economics

- Donkin, R., *Blood, Sweat and Tears: the Evolution of Work*. London: Texere, 2001.
- Dunleavy, P. and others, *Developments in British Politics* (latest edition). London: Macmillan, 2006.
- Easterlin, R., *The Reluctant Economist*. Cambridge: CUP, 2004.
- Hutton, W., *The World We're In*. London: Abacus, 2003.
- Toynbee, P., *Hard Work*. London: Bloomsbury, 2003.

British economic history

- Broadberry, S., and Solomou, S., *Protectionism and Economic Revival: The British Inter-war Economy.* Cambridge: CUP, 2008.
- Floud, R. and Johnson, P., eds, *The Cambridge Economic History of Modern Britain* (three vols). Cambridge: CUP, 2004.
- Hudson, P., *The Industrial Revolution.* London: Hodder, 1992.
- Mathias, P., *The First Industrial Nation.* Abingdon: Routledge, 2001.

UK, European and World history

- Clarke, P., *Hope and Glory.* London: Penguin, 2004.
- Diamond, J., *Guns, Germs and Steel.* London: Vintage, 2005.
- Hobsbawm, E., *Age of Extremes: the Short Twentieth Century 1914–1991*, London: Abacus, 1995.
- Judt, T., *PostWar.* London: Vintage, 2010.
- Landes, D.S., *The Wealth and Poverty of Nations: Why Are Some So Rich and Others So Poor?* New York, NY: Norton, 1999.
- Mazower, M., *Dark Continent: Europe's Twentieth Century.* London: Penguin, 2008.
- Vinen, R., *A History in Fragments: Europe in the Twentieth Century.* London: Abacus, 2002.

English

If you have a favourite author or authors and you mention them in your Personal Statement, be sure to have read as much of their work as possible. Know your author as well as their works. Investigate them as people, rather than only appreciating their writing. In addition, the following books are interesting works.

- Peter Barry, *Beginning Theory: An Introduction to Literary and Cultural Theory.*
- Jonathan Bate, *The Soul of the Age: Life, Mind and World of William Shakespeare.*
- Jonathan Culler, *Literary Theory: A Very Short Introduction.*
- Jonathan Culler, *On Deconstruction: Theory and Criticism after Structuralism.*
- Jonathan Culler, *Structuralist Poetics.*
- Jonathan Culler, *A Very Short Introduction to Critical Theory.*
- David Daiches, *Critical Approaches to English Literature.*
- Terry Eagleton, *Literary Theory: An Introduction.*
- Wilfred L. Guerin *et al.*, *A Handbook of Approaches to Literature.*
- Chris Hopkins, *Thinking About Texts: An Introduction to English Studies.*

- John Kerrigan, *Revenge Tragedy: From Aeschylus to Armageddon.*
- A.D. Nuttall, *Shakespeare The Thinker.*

Geography

Read the *National Geographic* magazine.

People, space, and geographies of difference

- Gough, J., Eisenschitz, A. and McCulloch, A., *Spaces of Social Exclusion.* Abingdon: Routledge, 2006.
- Held, D. (ed.), *A Globalising World? Culture, Economics, Politics*, 2nd edition. Abingdon: Routledge/Open University Press, 2004.

Historical geography

- Davis, M. *Late Victorian Holocausts: El Nino Famines and the Making of the Modern World Economy.* London: Verso, 2000.
- Graham, B. and Nash, C. (eds), *Modern Historical Geographies.* Harlow: Prentice Hall, 2000.
- Pomeranz, K., *The Great Divergence: China, Europe and the Making of the Modern World Economy.* Princeton, NJ: Princeton University Press, 2000.

Society, environment, and development

- Adams, W.M., *Green Development: Environment and Sustainability in the Third World*, 2nd edition. Abingdon: Routledge, 2001.
- Allen, T. and Thomas, A. (eds), *Poverty and Development into the 21st Century*, Oxford: OUP, 2000.
- Lawson, V., *Making Development Geography.* London: Hodder Arnold, 2007.

Physical geography (environmental processes and environmental change)

- Barry, R.G., Chorley, R.J. and Chase, T., *Atmosphere, Weather and Climate.* Abingdon: Routledge, 2003.
- Francis, P. and Oppenheimer, C., *Volcanoes.* Oxford: OUP, 2004.
- Gaston, K. and Spicer, J., *Biodiversity.* Oxford: Blackwell, 2nd edition, 2004.
- Masselink, G. and Hughes, M.G., *An Introduction to Coastal Processes and Geomorphology.* London: Hodder Arnold, 2003.

If you would like to buy something relevant to your geography course, two books which are highly recommended as being particularly useful are:

- Johnston, R. *et al.* (eds), *The Dictionary of Human Geography*, 4th edition. Chichester: Blackwell, 2000.
- Thomas, D. and Goudie, A. (eds), *The Dictionary of Physical Geography*, 3rd edition. Chichester: Blackwell, 2000.

History

The key piece of advice for would-be Oxbridge historians is to ensure that you have read widely around your A level topics. You need to show an awareness of recent historical debate and to understand different interpretations of the same events. The books listed below either deal with historiography or are particularly well written and deserve attention.

- Marc Bloch, *The Historian's Craft*.
- Peter Burke, *History and Social Theory*.
- C. Carpenter, *The Wars of the Roses*.
- E.H. Carr, *What is History?*
- C.S.L. Davies, *Peace, Print and Protestantism 1450–1558*.
- Geoffrey Elton, *The Practice of History*.
- Richard J. Evans, *In Defence of History*.
- J. Guy, *Tudor England*.
- E. Hallam, *Chronicles of the Age of Chivalry* and *Chronicles of the Wars of the Roses*.
- M.H. Keen, *England in the Later Middle Ages*.
- D.M. Loades, *Politics and the Nation 1450–1660*.
- Mark Mazower, *Dark Continent: Europe's Twentieth Century*.
- J. Sumption, *Trial by Battle* and *Trial by Fire*.

370-900

- J. Herrin, *The Formation of Christendom*.
- R. Hodges, and D. Whitehouse, *Mohammed, Charlemagne and the Origins of Europe*.
- J. Nelson, *Charles the Bald*.
- M. Whitlow, *The Making of Orthodox Byzantium, 600–1025*.

1000-1300

- R. Bartlett, *The Making of Europe: Conquest, Colonization and Cultural Change, 950–1350*.
- G. Holmes (ed.), *The Oxford Illustrated History of Medieval Europe*.
- R.W. Southern, *The Making of the Middle Ages*.

1400-1650

- A.G. Dickens, *Reformation and Society in Sixteenth Century Europe* and *The Counter Reformation*.
- G. Parker, *Europe in Crisis 1598–1648*.

1815-1914

- E.J. Hobsbawm, *The Age of Revolution 1789–1848*, *The Age of Capital 1848–1875*, and *The Age of Empire 1878–1914*.

Law

- Catherine Appleton, *Life after Life Imprisonment*.
- Marcel Berlins and Clare Dyer, *The Law Machine*.

- Lord Denning, *The Discipline of Law*.
- J.A.G. Griffith, *The Politics of the Judiciary*.
- Trevor Grove, *The Juryman's Tale*.
- Trevor Grove, *The Magistrate's Tale*.
- James A. Holland and Julian S. Webb, *Learning Legal Rules*.
- Michael J. Klarman, *Brown v. Board of Education and the Civil Rights Movement*.
- Nick McBride, *Letters to a Law Student*.
- Ian McLeod, *Legal Method*.
- John Pritchard, *The New Penguin Guide to the Law*.
- John Vidal, *McLibel: Burger Culture on Trial*.
- Jeremy Waldron, *The Law*.
- Glanville Williams, *Learning the Law*. (This is a popular introductory book. It will not give you any specific, substantive legal knowledge – but it will provide you with useful information ranging from how to read cases to what the abbreviations mean.)

Linguistics

- Akmajian, A., *Linguistics: An Introduction to Language and Communication*. Cambridge, MA: MIT Press, 2001.
- Atkinson, M., Kilby, D. and Roca, I., *Foundations of General Linguistics*. London: Unwin Hyman, 1988.
- Fromkin, V., Rodman, R. and Hyams, N., *An Introduction to Language*. Boston, MA: Thomson/Heinle, 2003.
- Newmeyer, F.J. (ed.), *Linguistics: The Cambridge Survey*. Cambridge: CUP, 1998.
- Radford, A., *Linguistics: An Introduction*. Cambridge: CUP, 1999.

Management

- Dixit, Avinash and Nalebuff, Barry, *Thinking Strategically: The Competitive Edge in Business, Politics, and Everyday Life*. New York, NY: W.W. Norton and Co, 1991.
- Handy, Charles, *Understanding Organisations*, 4th edition. London: Penguin, 1993.
- Pfeffer, Jeffery, *The Human Equation: Building Profits by Putting People First*. Watertown, MA: Harvard Business School Press, 1998.
- Pfeffer, Jeffery and Sutton, Robert, *Hard Facts, Dangerous Half-Truths and Total Nonsense: Profiting From Evidence-Based Management*. Boston, MA: Harvard Business School Press, 2006.
- McCraw, Thomas K., *Creating Modern Capitalism: How Entrepreneurs, Companies, and Countries Triumphed in Three Industrial Revolutions*. Watertown, MA: Harvard Business School Press, 1998.
- Tedlow, Richard, *New and Improved: The Story of Mass Marketing in America*. Maidenhead: McGraw-Hill, 1996.

Medicine

- Isaac Asimov, *New Guide to Science*.
- Bill Bryson, *A Short History of Nearly Everything*.
- W.H. Calvin and G. Ojemann, *Conversations with Neil's Brain*.
- Susan Greenfield, *The Human Brain: A Guided Tour*.
- Diarmuid Jeffreys, *Aspirin*.
- Dr Melvin Konner, *The Trouble with Medicine*.
- P.B. Medawar, *Advice to a Young Scientist*.
- Denis Noble, *The Music of Life*.
- Sherwin Nuland, *How We Die*.
- Sherwin Nuland, *How We Live*.
- Jo Revill, *Everything You Need to Know about Bird Flu*.
- Matt Ridley, *Genome*.
- Oliver Sacks, *The Man Who Mistook His Wife For a Hat*.
- David Seedhouse and Lisetta Lovett, *Practical Medical Ethics*.
- Lewis Thomas, *The Youngest Science*.
- James Watson, *DNA: The Secret of Life*.
- D.J. Weatherall, *Science and the Quiet Art*.
- Dr David Wilham, *Body Story*.

Podcasts

Oxford Podcasts: http://podcasts.ox.ac.uk

www.bbc.co.uk/sn

Radio 4 podcasts index: www.bbc.co.uk/radio4/programmes/genres/factual/scienceandnature

---

Modern languages

French: reading

- Albert Camus, *La Chute*.
- Marie Cardinal, *La Clé sur la Porte*.
- Gustave Flaubert, *Trois Contes*.
- André Gide, *La Porte Étroite*.
- François La Rochefoucauld, *Maximes*.
- Molière, *Le Misanthrope*.
- Marcel Proust, *Sur la Lecture*.
- Voltaire, *Candide* or *Micromegas* (short story).

French: films

Francois Truffaut, Robert Bresson, André Téchiné, Eric Rohmer, and Louis Malle are important figures in French cinema. Read the following texts if possible:

- Bresson, *Notes Sur le Cinématographe*.
- Truffaut, *Les Films de Ma Vie*.

German: reading

- Heinrich Böll, *Die Verlorene Ehre der Katharina Blum*.
- Bertolt Brecht, *Kaukasischer Kreidekreis; Mutter Courage*.
- Friedrich Dürrenmatt, *Die Physiker; Der Besuch der alten Dame*.
- Max Frisch, *Andorra*.
- Gunther Grass, *Die Blechtrommel; Katz und Maus*.
- Franz Kafka, *Die Verwandlung; Sämtliche Erzählungen*.
- Thomas Mann, *Tonio Kröger; Der Tod in Venedig*.
- Bernhard Schlink, *Der Vorleser*.
- Patrick Süskind, *Das Parfum; Die Taube*.

German: art

Taschen books are readily available and cheap. Read in English or German. Books are available on the following subjects:

- Expressionism
- Bauhaus
- Wiener Werkstätte.

German: films

Films about the Second World War:

- *Das Boot*.
- *Europa, Europa*.
- *Die Faelscher*.
- *Heimat*.
- *Sophie Scholl*.
- *Der Untergang*.

Films about the former East Germany:

- *Goodbye Lenin!*
- *Der Himmel über Berlin*.
- *Leben der Anderen*.
- *Sonnenallee*.
- *Der Tunnel*.

Italian: reading

- Italo Calvino, *Se una notte d'inverno un viaggiatore*.
- Natalia Ginzburg, *Lessico famigliare*.
- Tomasi di Lampedusa, *Il gattopardo*.
- Primo Levi, *Se questo è un uomo*.
- Luigi Pirandello, *Sei personaggi in cerca d'autore*.
- Leonardo Sciascia, *A ciascuno il suo*.
- Italo Svevo, *La coscienza di Zeno*.

Russian: reading

- Anna Akhmatova, *Requiem*.
- Iosif Brodsky, *Collected Poems in English 1972–1999*.
- Mikhail Bulgakov, *The Master and Margarita*.
- Ivan Bunin, *Life of Arseniev*.
- Anton Chekhov, *Uncle Vanya*.
- Fyodor Dostoevsky, *The Brothers Karamazov*.
- Nikolai Gogol, *Taras Bulba*.
- Mikhail Lermontov, *A Hero of our Time*.
- Boris Pasternak, *Doctor Zhivago*.
- Alexander Pushkin, *Eugene Onegin*.
- Aleksandr Solzhenitsyn, *One Day in the Life of Ivan Denisovich*.
- Leo Tolstoy, *Anna Karenina*.
- Ivan Turgenev, *A Month in the Country*.

Spanish: reading

- Leopoldo Alas, *La Regenta*.
- Pedro Calderón de la Barca, *La Vida es Sueño*.
- Pio Baroja, *El árbol de la Ciencia*.
- Camilo José Cela, *La Familia de Pascual Duarte*; *La Colmena*.
- Miguel de Cervantes, *El Quijote*.
- Julio Cortázar, *Rayuela*.
- Miguel Delibes, *Cinco Horas con Mario*.
- Rafael Sánchez Ferlosio, *El Jarama*.
- Carmen Martin Gaite, *Lo Raro es Vivir*.
- Juan Goytisolo, *Señas de Identidad*.
- Mario Vargas Llosa, *La Ciudad y los Perros*.
- Federico García Lorca, *Poeta en Nueva York*; *La Casa de Bernarda Alba*.
- Carlos Marcial, *El Surrealismo y Cuatro Poetas de la Generación del 27: (Ensayo Sobre Extensión y Límites Del Surrealismo en la Generación Del 27)*.
- Javier Marías, *Corazón Tan Blanco*.
- Gabriel Garcia Márquez, *Cien Años de Soledad*.
- Luis Martin-Santos, *Tiempo de Silencio*.
- Ana María Matute, *Olvidado Rey Gudú*.
- Eduardo Mendoza, *La Ciudad de los Prodigios*.
- Pablo Neruda, *Confieso Que he Vivido*.
- Fernando de Rojas, *La Celestina*.
- Miguel de Unamuno, *La Tía Tula*.

Spanish: films

- Pedro Almodóvar, *Todo Sobre mi Madre*.
- Jaime Chávarri, *Las Bicicletas son Para el Verano*.
- Víctor Erice, *El Espíritu de la Colmena*.
- Alejandro González Iñárritu, *Amores Perros; La Caza*.
- Carlos Saura, *Cría Cuervos; Elisa, Vida Mía*.

Music

In addition to reading you should become familiar with the Dover scores of string quartets and symphonies by Haydn, Mozart, and Beethoven. Aim to get to know several quartets and symphonies by all three composers.

- Aldwell, Edward and Schachter, Carl, *Harmony and Voice Leading*, 3rd edition. Belmont, CA: Wadsworth Publishing Co, 2002.
- Bohlman, Philip, *World Music: A Very Short Introduction*. Oxford: OUP, 2002.
- Caplin, William E., *Classical Form: A Theory of Formal Functions for the Instrumental Music of Haydn, Mozart, and Beethoven*. Oxford: OUP, 1998. This will be invaluable not only for your Analysis studies but also for your understanding of classical-period harmony.
- Clayton, Martin, Herbert, Trevor and Middleton, Richard, (eds), *The Cultural Study of Music: A Critical Introduction*. Abingdon: Routledge, 2003.
- Cook, Nicholas, *A Guide to Musical Analysis*. Oxford: OUP, 1994.
- Cook, Nicholas, *Music: A Very Short Introduction*. Oxford: OUP, 2000.
- Ledbetter, David, (ed.) *Continuo Playing According to Handel*. Wotton-Under-Edge: Clarendon Press, 1990.
- Morris, R.O., and Ferguson, Howard, *Preparatory Exercises in Score Reading*. Oxford: OUP, 1931.
- Parker, Roger, (ed.) *The Oxford Illustrated History of Opera*. Oxford: OUP, 1994.
- *The New Harvard Dictionary of Music*, Cambridge, MA: Harvard University Press, 1986; or *The Grove Concise Dictionary of Music*. London: Macmillan, 1988. Both are useful reference books.

Harmony and counterpoint

Play and study the following:

- *The Chorale Harmonisations of J.S. Bach*. Recommended edition: Breitkopf and Härtel, ed. B.F. Richter; less good but adequate: Chappell, ed Albert Riemenschneider.
- *Fugal Expositions by J.S. Bach in the Well-tempered Clavier (the '48')*. Recommended edition: Associated Board, ed. Richard Jones.
- *Schubert Lieder*. Recommended edition: Dover (either *Schubert's Songs to Texts* by Goethe or *Complete Song Cycles*). The Lieder of Beethoven, Mendelssohn, and Schumann are also recommended for your attention.
- Renaissance polyphony. Listen to some of the many fine recordings of the music of Palestrina and his contemporaries (the Gimell and Hyperion labels are a rich source).

Natural science (Cambridge)

Biology of cells

- Alberts, B. *et al.*, *Molecular Biology of the Cell*. Abingdon: Taylor & Francis, 2008.

Computer science

- Dewdney, A.K., *The New Turing Omnibus*. New York, NY: Computer Sciences Press, 1993 (reprinted 2001, Henry Holt).
- Körner, Tom W., *The Pleasures of Counting*. Cambridge: CUP, 1996.

Evolution and behaviour

- Barton, N.H. *et al.*, *Evolution*. Woodbury, NY: Cold Spring Harbour Lab. Press, 2007.
- Dawkins, R., *The Ancestor's Tale: A Pilgrimage to the Dawn of Life*. London: Weidenfeld & Nicolson, 2004.

Chemistry

- Atkins, P.W., *Atkin's Molecules*. Cambridge: CUP, 2003.
- Keeler, J. and Wothers, P., *Why Chemical Reactions Happen*. Oxford: OUP, 2003.

Geology (earth sciences)

- Benton, M.J., *When Life Nearly Died*. London: Thames & Hudson, 2005.
- Ince, M., *Rough Guide to the Earth*. London: Rough Guides/Penguin, 2007.

Materials science

- Ball, P., *Made to Measure: New Materials for the 21st Century*. Princeton, NJ: Princeton University Press, 1997.
- Cotterill, R.M.J., *The Material World*. Cambridge: CUP, 2008.
- Gordon, J.E., *New Science of Strong Materials*. London: Penguin, 1991.

Physiology of organisms

- King, J., *Reaching for the Sun*. Cambridge: CUP, 1997.
- Widmaier, E.P., *Why Geese Don't Get Obese (And We Do)*. New York, NY: WH Freeman, 2000.

Mathematics

- Gower, T., *Mathematics: A Very Short Introduction*. Oxford: OUP, 2002.
- Körner, Tom W., *The Pleasures of Counting*. Cambridge: CUP, 1996.
- Sivia, D.S. and Rawlings, S.G., *Foundations of Science Mathematics*. Oxford: OUP, 1999.

Elementary mathematics

- Foster, P.C., *Easy Mathematics for Biologists*. Abingdon: CRC, 1999.
- Huff, D., *How to Lie with Statistics*. London: Penguin, 1991.
- Rowntree, D., *Statistics Without Tears – An Introduction for Non-mathematicians*. London: Penguin, 2000.

Philosophy

- Alexander, H.G., *The Leibniz–Clarke Correspondence*.
- Ayer, A.J., *The Central Questions of Philosophy*.
- Blackburn, S., *Think: A Compelling Introduction to Philosophy*.
- Craig, E., *Philosophy: A Very Short Introduction*.
- Dancy, J., *An Introduction to Contemporary Epistemology*.
- Descartes, R., *Discourse on the Method* (many translations).
- Hodges, W., *Logic*.
- Hollis, M., *Invitation to Philosophy*.
- Hospers, J., *An Introduction to Philosophical Analysis*.
- Mill, J. S., *Utilitarianism*.
- Nagel, T., *What Does it all Mean?*.
- O'Hear, A., *What Philosophy Is: An Introduction to Contemporary Philosophy*.
- Russell, B., *The Problems of Philosophy*.
- Warburton, N., *Philosophy: The Basics*.
- Warburton, N., *Philosophy: The Classics*.

Politics

- Crick, Bernard, *Democracy: A Very Short Introduction*. Oxford: OUP, 2002.
- Dunn, John, *Western Political Theory in The Face of the Future*, revised edition. Cambridge: CUP, 1992.
- Geuss, Raymond, *History and Illusion*. Cambridge: CUP, 2000.
- Runciman, David, *The Politics of Good Intentions: History, Fear and Hypocrisy in the New World Order*. Princeton, NJ: Princeton University Press, 2006.
- Vieira, Monica Brito and Runciman, David, *Representation*. Cambridge: Polity Press, 2008.

Psychology

- Rita Carter, *Mapping the Mind*.
- Hugh Coolican, *Introduction to Research Methods and Statistics in Psychology*.
- Sigmund Freud, *The Psychopathology of Everyday Life*.

- Daniel Goleman, *Emotional Intelligence*.
- Richard D. Gross, *Psychology: The Science of Mind and Behaviour*.
- Nicky Hayes, *Foundations of Psychology: Introductory Text*.
- Miles Hewstone, Frank Fincham and Jonathan Foster, *Psychology*; *British Psychology*.
- Michael Hogg and Graham Vaughan, *Social Psychology: An Introduction*.
- Allan Pease, *Body Language*.
- H. Rudolf Schaffer, *Introducing Child Psychology*; *Concepts in Developmental Psychology*.
- Robert Winston, *The Human Mind*.

The Psychologist, a monthly publication of the British Psychological Society, has back issues freely available on its archive at www.thepsychologist.org.uk.

Sociology

- Alexander, J.C. and Thompson, K., *A Contemporary Introduction to Sociology: Culture and Society in Transition*. London/Boulder, CO: Paradigm Publishers, 2008.
- Crompton, R., *Class and Stratification*, 3rd edition. Cambridge: Polity Press, 2008.
- Giddens, A., *Sociology*, 6th edition. Cambridge: Polity Press, 2009.
- Sennett, R., *The Culture of the New Capitalism*. London: Yale University Press, 2006.

Statistics

- Graham, A., *Teach Yourself Statistics*. Maidenhead: McGraw-Hill, 2008.
- Huff, D., *How to Lie with Statistics*. London: Penguin, 1991.
- Rowntree, D., *Statistics Without Tears – An Introduction for Non-mathematicians*. London: Penguin, 2000.

Further resources

In addition to the suggestions above, remember to:

- read around your subject in the press
- search for podcasts and videos
- check out blogs and online articles.

5 | Experience to support your application

When you apply to Oxbridge, you are required to be a step above candidates applying to other universities. As discussed in the previous chapter, you need to have read widely in your subject area. One way to prepare even more thoroughly is through additional experience outside school life. You may wish to take a gap year to improve a language, for example, and this chapter considers the pros and cons of taking time out.

Work experience is essential if you think you want to study a vocational subject such as law or medicine, and you should think about organising this in your summer holiday the year before you apply. In addition, it is important to keep your eyes and ears open to relevant events that you can attend in your area, newspaper articles that relate to your subject, blogs, radio programmes, and any other sources of information that might give your application an additional dimension.

Gap years

Policies about taking gap years vary from college to college, and from subject to subject, so it is important that you discuss your plans with the admissions tutor at your chosen college well in advance of your application. If you want to study a subject where languages are helpful (art history, history, music, and modern languages, to name only four), then taking a gap year to improve your fluency in a second or third language may give you a distinct advantage. On the other hand, if you are applying for maths, admissions tutors may be afraid that you will forget your A level knowledge during the year out and be reluctant to accept you. If you do decide to take a gap year it is absolutely essential that you make concrete and creative plans. Admissions tutors will want to see proof of your experiences in your Personal Statement, and at interview, and will expect your time to have been spent constructively in a way that will enhance your university studies.

You also need to decide whether to make an application for deferred entry (this is when you apply whilst doing your A levels, two years in advance of your first term at university) or to apply a year after your school friends do, whilst you are on your year out. When making this decision you should ring your college of choice to discuss their preferences. Some Cambridge and Oxford colleges do not like making offers to deferred entrants, simply because this means they have to commit a place before they have met competing applicants for the following year. In this case colleges encourage you to wait a year and apply whilst on your gap year. If you ask their advice and make the most of your time out you can guarantee that you will not be penalised. In allowing yourself time to mature you may even make a better application and become a more attractive candidate.

As the Cambridge prospectus explains:

'About one in five students coming to Cambridge take a gap year before starting their studies. This year out proves a very useful time in which to improve skills, earn money, travel and generally gain maturity and self-reliance.'

Cambridge Prospectus, 2008–9

Work experience

Work experience can be a great way to explore the subject you hope to study at university. Experience within the work environment is particularly important if you want to study a vocational subject, for example law or medicine. It is often only in a work situation that you can fully understand the stresses, responsibilities, and pleasures that go along with a particular career, and only then can you really commit. Work experience can provide admissions tutors with strong evidence that candidates are committed, determined, and have thought their applications through carefully. It can also provide you with a goal that keeps you motivated even through the toughest periods of study.

Apart from having a real idea of where you might end up in five years' time, work experience can expose you to ideas related to the subject you are about to study in exciting ways. For example, if you want to study natural sciences at Cambridge, try to get a week during school holidays helping or observing at a laboratory where the scientists are working on something you are particularly interested in. You will be able to sit in on lab meetings and hear for yourself the problems that they face and the solutions they come to. You can also ask them personally for reading suggestions. No one will be as ahead of the game as they will and this will give you some really exciting things to discuss at interview.

Above are only three examples of subjects where work experience is helpful but this is applicable to any subject. If you are really serious about studying and learning, find a way to get more information within the work environment. This will not only give you greater knowledge and confidence, it will also show the admissions tutors that you are really interested. Remember, however, work experience should be directly relevant to your chosen subject.

Organising work experience can take several months; patience and persistence are necessary, particularly in the economic climate of today. Statistically, the most successful method of finding these placements – indeed in finding jobs after university – is through networking: asking friends and family. Tell everyone you know what you are planning to do at university and what you are particularly interested in and ask if they know anyone who might give you a hand. Second, target institutions, departments, and companies directly. If you have a contact there, ring him or her, otherwise ring the HR department. Do ring, don't just send them a letter, since people are more likely to remember your voice than an envelope or email. Once you have spoken to someone in person tell them you are going to send them a follow-up email with your CV and a cover letter. Write the email and send it immediately. Then ring them back a few days later to ask whether they have received your letter and email, and whether they have any task to give you.

Case study: Tracy, Natural Sciences, Oxford

Since coming to study in England my ambition has been to study chemistry at Oxford. I knew that I needed to get some work experience during the summer before I applied so that I would have something unusual to say when I got to the interview, and something meaty to add to my Personal Statement. I come from Beijing, in China, so before I went home for the summer I contacted my parents and told them I needed some work experience. They spoke to their friends, and, magically, a friend of a friend had a contact with a research lab in my home city. When I went home for the summer I spent two weeks working in that research lab. It was really interesting, as they were developing some new chemicals that could be really helpful in developing drugs to cure terminal illnesses. I asked so many questions, and had the opportunity to help out a bit with their experiments. Mostly I watched, but that didn't matter. The experience really confirmed for me that I wanted to make science – and in particular chemistry – a career. I felt so passionate about it, and I guess the interviewers saw this, because I got a place!

Events in your area

If you want to study a humanities subject, particularly a subject that is not vocational, keeping up to date with current affairs and events in your area is perhaps even more important than work experience. If you are really passionate about your subject, and dedicated to getting a place at Oxford or Cambridge, you should be constantly on the lookout for events in your area that are relevant to the subject that you want to study. Local libraries often host talks by renowned authors, the Royal Institute and the Science Museum in London stage regular science lectures, the Royal Geographic Society organises regular discussions with eminent geographers, and the Royal Academy of Art has an ongoing art history lecture series. In addition, the universities in your area may hold lectures that could interest you. Speak to your teachers for ideas or go online to search for relevant events.

Ideas you might consider include:

- politics: go on a tour of the Houses of Parliament
- law: sit in the public gallery of your local magistrates' or Crown Court
- history and archaeology: visit the British Museum
- art and history of art: visit every gallery and museum you can get to, including the galleries local to Oxford and Cambridge.

You should also be aware of news stories that relate to developments in your field. Try to get as big a picture as possible about your subject: about how it relates to the rest of the word and why it might be important to know about it. Keep up to date with relevant blogs and think-tanks, read the newspapers online and listen to podcasts.

Case study: Ella, History, Oxford

When I was writing my Personal Statement for UCAS and preparing for my interview I spent hours reading articles in the press and visiting museums and historical sites. I was interested in the whole concept of 'history' and how it impacts on us in society and our everyday lives. I wanted to make sure that I had really thought deeply and philosophically about the subject I wanted to study, so that I wouldn't be caught out by strange interview questions, and so I had strong opinions of my own.

I visited quite a lot of museums in London, particularly the British Museum, and this helped to put in perspective just how subjective the telling of history can be. I mean, the British Museum is a collection of artefacts which were brought together when Britain was an empire. The grand building continues to create a picture of the UK as a powerful nation with intellectual superiority and political reach. And although things have changed since it was first open – slavery has been abolished, the colonies are no more – we continue to frame our past in the same way.

In addition to visiting exhibitions and museums I listened to radio broadcasts by historians and thinkers that opened my mind to different concepts, completely separate from anything I had thought about at school. The radio programme *In Our Time* is a favourite of mine. I also read the papers every day, and cut out any article that I thought was important. I realised that the political slants given in news stories by journalists could be seen in official history, and I came to consider history as a subjective narrative.

I hadn't had any relevant work experience when I was planning my application, so I wanted to do something practical that showed I could think on my feet. I had gone to a talk on 'British Identity' at the Tate Britain and was really excited about the idea that the notion of 'identity' could be something fluid and shaped by many different subjective historical narratives. I wanted to understand how 'history' shapes people's lives today. I wrote a questionnaire and took it first to all my friends and family, and then to neighbours and finally to friendly-looking people on the street. I got some really interesting answers.

Having my eyes open and consciously absorbing information from all around me was, I think, the reason I got an offer to start studying history in October 2009.

6 | Choosing your university and college

Deciding between Cambridge and Oxford may seem daunting, and you cannot apply to both. Most students have a gut feeling about where they want to go. You may have visited the cities as a tourist and found one more attractive than the other. You may also have gone to an open day at both universities and found one more friendly or welcoming. These are all perfectly good reasons for making your choice. If, however, you are still in a quandary, the following information may give you some help.

Choosing the university by subject

Choosing the university by subject is one way of simplifying matters. It is essential to check that the university you prefer teaches the subject you wish to study. There are various subjects that Oxford offers which Cambridge does not and vice versa.

Subjects you can study at Cambridge but not at Oxford include:

- architecture
- economics (as a stand-alone subject; in Oxford you do a combined course of economics and management)
- education studies
- land economy
- the languages Dutch, Anglo-Saxon, Norse, and Celtic
- management studies (as a stand-alone subject; in Oxford you do a combined course of economics and management)
- natural sciences (at Oxford all the sciences are offered but not in the same combination)
- philosophy (as a stand-alone subject; at Oxford you do a combined course of philosophy, politics and economics – PPE)
- social and political science (SPS)
- veterinary medicine.

Subjects you can study at Oxford but not at Cambridge include:

- the languages Sanskrit and Czech with Slovak
- philosophy, politics and economics (PPE)

- psychology, philosophy and physiology (PPP)
- separate sciences (although you do have to take modules in other science subjects as well).

Subjects you can study at both universities include:

- archaeology and anthropology
- classics
- computer science
- engineering
- English literature and language
- geography
- history
- human sciences
- law
- modern and medieval languages
- music
- oriental studies (at Oxford) and Asian and Middle Eastern studies (at Cambridge)
- theology and religious studies.

It is important to note that, although many courses have the same name, their components may differ between the two universities and you should take time to compare the courses in detail.

> For more information go to the websites listed below.
>
> - Cambridge: www.cam.ac.uk/admissions/undergraduate
> - Oxford: www.admissions.ox.ac.uk

Differences in course structure at Oxford and Cambridge

Comparing the Tripos system at Cambridge with the two-part system at Oxford can be another way to help you to decide which university is better suited to you. One of the great attractions of Cambridge is the flexibility of its Tripos system (the name Tripos is said to have been derived from the three-legged stool that undergraduates in the Middle Ages sat on for their oral examinations).

Each course, or Tripos, is usually divided into two parts: Part I and Part II. After each 'part' there is an exam that counts towards your final undergraduate mark. A 'Part I' can take one year (in economics, for example) or two years (in English). A two-year Part I is divided into Part IA and Part IB. Once you have completed Part I (A and B), you have the option of continuing to specialise in the same subject, or swapping to a related but different subject for Part II.

In theory this gives students quite a bit of flexibility, and there have been students who have studied three different related subjects during the course of their three years at Cambridge and come out with a First Class degree. In reality, however, you should not go to interview thinking that you will be able to change courses easily.

Admissions tutors, particularly those interviewing for humanities, arts, and social sciences, will see this as a sign that a student is not committed to their subject, and give the place to someone who is. If students want to change subject when they get to Cambridge they have to work very hard at convincing their existing DOS that they want to change for the right reasons. Then students have to convince a DOS in their new subject to take them on.

On the other hand, there are subjects where elongated undergraduate degrees are encouraged. Natural sciences and mathematics students have the option of adding a Part III, while engineering students take Parts IA, IB, IIA, and IIB over four years, leading ultimately to the award of MEng.

The system works slightly differently at Oxford. As at Cambridge, students have to pass exams in two parts. However, students do not have to take examinations at the end of each year, as is the case in many Cambridge courses. The Preliminary Examinations (or 'Prelims') are taken at the end of the first year (except for experimental psychology and PPP, where they are taken at the end of the second term), and the Final Examinations ('Finals') are taken at the end of the third year. So most undergraduates at Oxford University do not take exams in their second year.

In general there are more courses at Oxford which are designed to take four years. The Joint Honours courses of mathematics and philosophy and physics and philosophy, as well as classics, take four years. Mathematics itself, physics, and earth sciences can take either three or four years (your choice), but in the case of molecular and cellular biochemistry, chemistry, engineering, and metallurgy, students are normally expected to progress to the fourth research-based year leading to the award of the master's degree.

You should research the similarities and differences as they apply to your particular subject choice carefully, and then be prepared to discuss your discoveries when it comes to interview.

Choosing the right college

Oxford has 30 colleges and six permanent private halls and Cambridge has 29 colleges, so there is a lot of choice. When deciding upon a college it can be tempting to choose strategically. Students often think that if they apply to an undersubscribed college they will have a higher chance of securing a place. However, in practice, this is not the case.

Competition for places is regulated by subject rather than college (for example, at Cambridge there are 10 architecture applicants for each place, five economics applicants per place, and two applicants for each place studying education). Nor does your college choice make any difference to the quality of the teaching you will receive. All students attend lectures at the faculty and have supervisions at various different colleges depending on where the teaching staff and experts are based. The college is, above all, the place where you will be living over the next three years and therefore it is most sensible to make your decision according to where you think you will be most at home.

The obvious way to get a feel for a college is to visit it. Have a wander round, talk to the porters at the front gate, and let them know that you are thinking of applying. They will almost certainly have stories to tell and advice to give. Alternatively you can visit the colleges on an official open day, where you can meet other applicants and some of the college fellows. For information about open days go to the websites below.

- Cambridge: www.cam.ac.uk/admissions/undergraduate/opendays
- Oxford: www.ox.ac.uk/admissions/undergraduate_courses/open_days

Another way to find out about a college is to pick up the phone and have a chat with the admissions tutor. If he or she sounds friendly and welcoming it is a sure sign that you will be made to feel at home.

To get the telephone numbers of different colleges and to get more information, look at the university prospectuses as well as the individual college prospectuses. These can also be downloaded online at the addresses below.

- Cambridge: www.cam.ac.uk/admissions/undergraduate/publications/prospectus
- Oxford: www.ox.ac.uk/admissions/prospectuses.html

In addition, each Junior Common Room (JCR) produces a student-written 'alternative prospectus'; this is less formal and gives you the student perspective on the college. Again, contact the college or ask for the email of the JCR president to order a copy. All prospectuses will be sent to you free of charge. You can also download these alternative prospectuses from the addresses below.

- Cambridge: www.cusu.cam.ac.uk/prospective/prospectus
- Oxford: www.ousu.org/prospective-students

While you visit the colleges and read the prospectuses, there are a number of factors that you should consider in order to make a good college choice. Some of these factors are academic, others are personal, and all are equally important. Make sure you consider the points below.

1. **Whether the college offers your subject.** Not all colleges offer every subject, so this is the first thing to find out. Oxford produces a table that summarises this information at www.admissions.ox.ac.uk/colleges/availab. For Cambridge you will have to look at each college separately.
2. **The size of the college.** Small colleges often feel more cosy and you are more likely to get to know all your peers. In large colleges you will feel more anonymous but will have a wealth of new people to meet.
3. **The distance from the college to the centre of town and your faculty.** It is often overlooked, but a 20-minute cycle ride from college to a faculty lecture in the pouring rain can be extremely unpleasant. On the other hand, colleges further from the centre tend to have larger grounds for sport, and more of a communal atmosphere.
4. **Whether the college offers accommodation for the duration of your studies.** Some colleges only provide accommodation for the first year and you are expected to find a house after that. Some people like living in a house with their friends but there are associated problems, for example unhelpful landlords and houses that are far away from your college.
5. **The size and facilities of the accommodation available.** Most college accommodation consists of a single room, perhaps with an en suite bathroom, but more usually shared bathrooms on one staircase. Some colleges have gyms, some have practice rooms for musicians, some have neither.
6. **The politics of entrance.** The ratio of students who come from state or private schools, between men and women, and between traditional entrants and ethnic minorities differs from college to college. These figures are given on each college's prospectus. You may need to take into consideration the political leanings of a college. Some colleges are very left wing (King's College, Cambridge, for example) and accept less than average numbers of privately schooled applicants. Others are happy to accept students from private schools. The reputation of a college is worth researching for this reason.

The colleges at Oxford and Cambridge are ranked regularly, showing the relative academic success of their students in their final exams. These tables are included below, and you may wish to look at them. At Oxford the league table is called the Norrington Table (Table 1) and at Cambridge it is called the Tompkins Table (Table 2). Degrees obtained at the college are scored in the following way: five points for a First; three for a 2:1; two for a 2:2, and one for a Third. The scores shown in Tables 1 and 2 are the percentages of total points available. Studying these tables is useful purely because they offer a list of all the colleges in each university. However, they should be used with caution. Remember, every college belongs to Oxbridge and therefore is highly regarded by the outside world. If you

Table 1: Oxford University Norrington Table 2009–10

College	Score	Rank
Magdalen	79.45%	1
Corpus Christi	75.59%	2
Merton	75.00%	3
St John's	73.69%	4
New	73.09%	5
University	71.96%	6
Christ Church	71.67%	7
Worcester	70.78%	8
Balliol	70.38%	9
Jesus	70.11%	10
Oriel	69.87%	11
Hertford	69.75%	12
Wadham	69.68%	13
St Catherine's	69.22%	14
Lincoln	69.11%	15
Queen's	68.86%	16
Pembroke	68.18%	17
St Anne's	67.90%	18
St Hugh's	67.89%	19
Lady Margaret Hall	67.19%	20
St Hilda's	67.03%	21
Brasenose	66.53%	22
St Edmund Hall	66.42%	23
Somerville	66.41%	24
Trinity	66.30%	25
St Peter's	65.83%	26
Exeter	65.68%	27
Keble	65.65%	28
Mansfield	63.16%	29
Harris Manchester	60.95%	30

Reprinted with kind permission of the University of Oxford.

go to a higher ranking college this does not mean you will receive better tuition, although it may mean that the environment at the college will be more intense: something that is not always enjoyable.

These rankings should be treated with caution, since the number of degrees awarded per college is small and the results are dependent on the performance of a particular group of students in a particular year. The University of Oxford does not recommend that students base their college choice on such rankings.

Table 2: Cambridge University Tompkins Table 2010

Rank (Previous year's rank)	College	Score	Percentage of Firsts attained
1 (2)	Emmanuel	69.11%	33.2%
2 (1)	Trinity	67.15%	32.1%
3 (7)	Churchill	67.08%	29.0%
4 (9)	Trinity Hall	66.02%	25.1%
5 (8)	Magdalene	65.31%	24.3%
6 (3)	Selwyn	64.88%	23.7%
7 (16)	Peterhouse	64.85%	27.0%
8 (18)	Clare	64.19%	23.5%
9 (5)	St Catharine's	64.15%	23.8%
10 (6)	Pembroke	64.04%	24.1%
11 (4)	Gonville & Caius	63.72%	24.2%
12 (13)	Christ's	63.62%	22.0%
13 (10)	Corpus Christi	63.48%	21.6%
14 (17)	King's	62.69%	23.4%
15 (15)	Downing	62.42%	18.6%
16 (11)	Jesus	62.32%	19.7%
17 (12)	Queens'	62.16%	22.6%
18 (22)	Sidney Sussex	61.86%	20.3%
19 (19)	Robinson	61.79%	18.3%
20 (14)	St John's	61.73%	19.1%
21 (20)	Girton	60.38%	16.4%
22 (21)	Fitzwilliam	59.56%	16.2%
23 (23)	Murray Edwards	59.53%	14.3%
24 (27)	Wolfson	59.51%	10.9%
25 (24)	Newnham	58.73%	14.2%
26 (25)	Homerton	58.65%	14.6%
27 (26)	Hughes Hall	57.98%	16.4%
28 (28)	St Edmund's	54.68%	8.0%
29 (29)	Lucy Cavendish	52.45%	11.7%

The *Independent*, Friday, 9 July 2010

Open applications

If you are still unsure about which college is for you, there is the option of making an open application. This is an application where you do not specify a college on your UCAS form; instead, the admissions computer will assign you to a college that is undersubscribed in your subject. Approximately 15% of students applying to Oxbridge make open applications, and the success rates are the same as for college-specific applications. Obviously, if there is a college that you really do not want to go to it is a bad idea to apply in this way, since you may be assigned to the very college you want to avoid. However, an open application may be a good way to settle your doubts, and most students end up loving their college, even if it was not their first choice. The following two statements made by admissions tutors from Oxford and Cambridge may help to put your mind at rest.

> *'If an applicant makes an open application and the statistical programme allocates that candidate to our college, the candidate will be treated as if they applied directly to our college.'*
> *Admissions Tutor, Cambridge, 2010*

> *'Cooperative arrangements between the colleges are designed to ensure that able candidates applying to oversubscribed college are placed at other colleges. Almost 20% of successful candidates are placed at a college other than their college of preference each year.'*
> *Oxford Prospectus*

7 | UCAS and the Personal Statement

Applying to Oxford and Cambridge happens in the same way as applying to any other university: through the Universities and Colleges Admissions Service (UCAS). The UCAS form is a long document that is completed online and sent to all five of your chosen universities by 15 October. (For more advice about completing the UCAS form, see Appendix 3). It asks you to include details of your school(s), exam grades, employment experience, your choices of university in order of preference, and a Personal Statement: a 47-line (or 4,000 character) written document that outlines the reasons for your choice of subject.

Because most young people who apply to Oxbridge will have excellent grades (usually A*AAA at A level) as well as a glowing report from their teachers, the UCAS Personal Statement is very important. This piece of writing provides the admissions tutor with the first glimpse of your personality and intellect, and is the closest thing they have to meeting you until the interviews in December. This is also the first example of your written work that they will see. Your Personal Statement needs to stand out from the piles of similar documents strewn across the admissions tutor's desk. You need to come across as someone they – and their colleagues – would be happy to teach for many hours. The Personal Statement, therefore, plays a large part in their decision about whether or not to invite you to interview.

What qualities are the admissions tutors looking for?

When the admissions tutor reads your Personal Statement, there are some very specific qualities he or she will look for. These qualities are listed below.

1. *Proof that you have made an appropriate subject choice*
2. *An ability to survive in an intense and pressured atmosphere*
3. *A depth of interest in the subject*
4. *An ability to study independently.*

Admissions Tutor, Cambridge

What exactly do the admissions tutors mean by this?

1. They want to see that you have thought long and hard about what you want to study and why; that you have investigated the subject fully, through extensive reading.
2. Pressure is high at Oxbridge, and students who apply to either Cambridge or Oxford must be prepared for this. Admissions tutors need to be sure that you are someone who will flourish in the intense environment. Not everyone does. If you have survived the pressures of multiple A level courses and exams, this is already a good sign. If, in addition, you show that you have been able to juggle several extra-curricular activities as well as undertaking research towards your university subject, then admissions tutors will recognise that you are a resilient student with stamina.
3. Depth of interest in your subject is essential, as discussed previously. If you show that you have made a serious effort to read around your subject this sends positive signals to the admissions tutor. Even better, if you show that, whilst reading, you found an area within your discipline that interests you particularly, and then you have followed this up further with more in-depth study, you will have shown that you can undertake university-level research and are deeply committed to your subject.
4. If you have read above and beyond what your teachers have given you in class, you are showing proof of independent study that will be essential when you go to university. This also shows a deeper commitment to your subject and good studentship.

A model Personal Statement

There are no hard and fast rules about how to structure your Personal Statement. Below, however, is an example of how a well-organised statement might be written with a synopsis, paragraph by paragraph. Below each synopsis is an example of a paragraph written by a candidate who did get an interview at Cambridge to read economics. Read the example carefully, but do not be tempted to copy it.

The first paragraph should be punchy and attention-grabbing. It should explain, in as few sentences as possible, why you are so excited to study your chosen subject and why you think it is worth studying.

> Physics answers the question of why? Maths is a tool to solve quantitative issues. Politics is the study of the structure of law, government and policy. Economics, as I see it, is everything in between.

In paragraph two you could discuss your particular interests in relation to your university subject choice. This is your chance to write about specific ideas you have developed as a result of reading beyond your A level syllabus, any visits that have inspired you, or work experience that has opened your mind to new ideas. Paragraphs one and two should take up about two-thirds of the entire statement.

I thoroughly enjoy and am extremely interested in economics. The distinct view on the world that economists have and the power to do good are the reasons why I am so enthused about the subject. I'm particularly drawn to development economics, but acknowledge the role that other spheres of economics such as econometrics, micro- and macroeconomics play in the constitution of this field. This is why my current goal as a student of economics is to learn as much about the subject in general. To this end, I have read several works of prominent economists, delving into mind-expanding texts such as 'Development as Freedom', 'Capitalism and Freedom', 'Globalisation and its Discontents' and Adam Smith's 'Wealth of Nations'. In addition to my individual exploration, I have attended courses at Harvard University and at Brown University for Economics and Global Development respectively.

The third paragraph can start to incorporate your personal experiences and how these have shaped your academic interests and choice of university subject.

My passion for economics, especially development economics, comes as a result of my background and experiences. I have been fortunate enough to travel, experience different cultures, lifestyles and perspectives. Seeing suffering and poverty through community service has made me internalise these issues. Possessing a heritage that combines both economically developed and developing nations (as I have lived in both Costa Rica and Britain) has underlined this problem for me. Throughout my life, I have seen myself as a problem-solver and I believe this has been highlighted through Young Enterprise. Being Head of Production, I was in charge of overcoming difficulties such as rising costs. We did not win in the end, but it was a great learning experience and one that showed me the importance of thinking creatively.

The fourth paragraph can include a brief summary of your extra-curricular activities. Remember, the admissions tutor will have to live with you for three years if you get in to his or her college. You need to come across as a responsible, friendly person who will be an asset, rather than an embarrassment, to the college's reputation. Finish off with a closing sentence that reminds the reader why you want to study the subject you have chosen.

> Aside from travelling and learning, I appreciate the arts and sports greatly. Acting is a passion of mine and started by attending Theatre Saturday School at the age of six. Since then I have been involved in different types of work, for instance, I was involved with a professional children's production which produced the play 'Annie' and I played the lead male role. Economics, however, has developed into my newest and greatest interest as it seems to combine not only all my academic endeavours but also permeates my pursuits out of the classroom.

When you have finished writing your Personal Statement, get your parents, older siblings, and teachers to check it. Make sure there are no spelling errors and ask the people who read it whether it sounds like it was written by you. It is, after all, you who will be going to meet the admissions tutors, and you who want to be accepted by Oxbridge. Do not be tempted to plagiarise. Both universities have a computer system to spot plagiarism, and will automatically reject you if you have done this. Make sure, also, that you are prepared to discuss every piece of information in your Personal Statement if you are called to interview. Admissions tutors will almost certainly pick up on any books you say you have read as a conversation-starter; so read them all again.

Extra-curricular experiences in the Personal Statement: keeping everything relevant

It is a good idea to discuss extra-curricular activities and work experience that is relevant to your chosen degree. It is very important that you weave these experiences into a discussion about why you want to study your subject. All the information you include must form part of a life story that seems to lead directly to your chosen undergraduate degree at Oxbridge.

Below is a very good example of paragraph two from one student's Personal Statement. Her name is Laura, and she was asked to interview at Cambridge for medicine.

I organised some work experience in the orthopaedic wing of Nottingham Hospital and at my local GP clinic. At Nottingham Hospital, I shadowed the doctors on their ward round, watched a number of knee replacements and observed fracture clinic which made me realise how such a simple procedure can dramatically increase the quality of life in older people. This is such a stark contrast with my experiences in Uganda where living to 70 is seen as something of a miracle. A further thing I learnt from my work experience is the importance of patient–doctor relationships, and this is one of the factors which really draws me to medicine. I saw this most particularly in my work experience with a GP where I saw him take on a central role of trust within the community. I have had much opportunity to develop my interpersonal skills. During sixth form I worked with underprivileged children at an after-school club in London. I have volunteered in a charity shop and this year I am volunteering one day a week at St Peter's Hospice in Green Town. I am able to easily relate to people and enjoy meeting, getting to know and trying to help different people. I used this skill when I was deputy head girl of my school, where I was involved in talking to students and helping them with any problems they might have. I keep up to date with the news, reading about medical developments in the 'BMJ' and the 'New Scientist'.

Not only is Laura's work experience specifically relevant to medicine, but she has woven her experiences into a narrative that explains very clearly why she wants to study this subject at university and why she would be good at it.

Following is one more Personal Statement in its entirety. The author, Imogen, applied to Oxford to read French and Italian. She was invited to interview. (Character count: 3,025).

In a world where increasing numbers of people speak English, it may seem superfluous for students to put their efforts into acquiring foreign languages. For me, however, language is not just a means by which we communicate, but the barrier of language often hides whole worlds of literature and culture which can remain inaccessible, even through translation. For this reason, language as a whole is a source of fascination for me, resulting in a desire to focus on Italian, which I studied at A level, and French, a language I very much enjoyed at GCSE and which I feel complements Italian well. I have therefore resolved to take a one-year French A level course during my gap year, enabling me to study it at university.

I think literature portrays language at its best, as it is the means by which a language displays the full range of its versatility and the essence of the people who communicate through it. It often offers a window into the culture it describes, which I feel is especially well achieved by Natalia Ginzburg. After studying 'Le Voci della Sera' at A level, I read 'La Strada che Va in Citte' and 'E Stato Cosi', finding that her depiction of the various female characters strongly impresses upon the reader the difficulties faced by these women in the light of their religion and community. One sympathises easily with them as they struggle to find happiness, owing largely to Ginzburg's simple and often stark narrative. Similarly, I admire Primo Levi for the style in which he narrates, maintaining a dignified approach to the experiences he describes. In 'Se Non Ora, Quando?' his depiction of Italy is striking: an oasis of freedom, where Jews and Christians are indistinguishable.

To help improve my French I have read various works of literature and philosophy. I became interested in the problem of evil through my Philosophy A level, so I read Voltaire's 'Zadig', which demonstrates how suffering is unavoidable, but that sense and perseverance will see a man through. This, however, does little to solve the theological problem of evil. Nor does 'Candide' 12 years later, but it highlights flaws in the ideology that 'tout est au mieux', or 'all is for the best', and points forward to suggest how to live happily in spite of evil. I subscribe to the literary magazine 'Virgule', through which I discovered Pierre de Ronsard, in whom I was delighted to find traces of Petrarch, by whom I have read some 'Canzoniere', and numerous classical authors that I have studied. I read a selection of 'Les Amours', and found that there was much opportunity for intertextual comparison with the texts I have studied in the past.

Last summer I worked as an au pair in France, which improved my French enormously, not only giving me an understanding of French daily life, but also valuable experience of the world of work. At school I was awarded the Prize for Classics and Italian, for linguistic success and contribution to these areas. Outside academic concerns, I was a Managing Director of a Young Enterprise company in Year 12, and have completed the Silver Duke of Edinburgh's award, as well as a qualification in youth leadership, which I hope have made me responsible and motivated. In addition to playing the piano, I sang in two choirs at school and continue to take lessons, focusing on Italian arias. Alongside my studies this year, I follow Italian current affairs by transcribing the TG2 news, and am taking conversation classes weekly. I am also taking classes at the Institut Français in London to help me become more fluent in French, and shall continue to read avidly, exploring as many authors as possible.

Additional form for Cambridge: the Supplementary Application Questionnaire (SAQ)

Once you have completed your Personal Statement and sent off your UCAS form, the Cambridge Admissions Office will automatically email you an additional questionnaire to complete: the SAQ. The SAQ is filled out online, costs nothing to send, and gives Cambridge more information about you and your application. If you do not have access to email you can contact the Cambridge Admissions Office for a paper version.

The initial email will give you all the information you need in order to complete the form correctly, as well as a deadline (usually the end of October).

The SAQ includes the following eight sections.

1. **Photograph.** You will need a passport-sized colour photograph of yourself, preferably in digital format, which can then be uploaded onto the form.
2. **Application type.** This section asks questions about your application, such as whether you have applied for an organ scholarship, if you are taking a gap year, or whether you are going through the Special Access Scheme.
3. **Personal details.** This covers information about you and your own situation, such as where you live, what your first name is, etc.
4. **Course details.** Here you need to declare your preferred course options (if applicable); for example, if you are applying to read modern and medieval languages, you state which languages you wish to study in this section.
5. **Education.** In this section, you will need to give information about your school(s), such as class sizes and descriptions of any extra help you may have received towards your application.
6. **Qualifications.** In this section, you need to give details of your AS and/or A level modules, or their equivalents, and your marks.
7. **Additional information.** This is where you can add an additional Personal Statement. You will also need to discuss your career plans and give some proof of your interest in your chosen subject (for example, details of your work experience).
8. **Submit.**

The additional Personal Statement is the perfect opportunity for you to explain to the admissions tutor how excited you are about the course and perhaps the college to which you are applying. Do take advantage of this extra space to make an impression.

Remember, however, not to duplicate anything you have said on the UCAS form. While your UCAS Personal Statement will be seen by every institution you apply to, the SAQ is for the admissions tutors at Cambridge only. This means that you can discuss particular elements of the course content or programme at Cambridge without putting any other university off. Make the most of this and explain why their course and teaching staff are perfect for you, and why you will fit in particularly well there.

Remember also that by mentioning your areas of special academic interest, you will encourage predictable questions at interview, making it easier to prepare thoroughly. Here is a good example written by a student for his economics application.

I am particularly interested in studying economics at Cambridge as the faculty stresses its commitment to public policy, and I share the view of its importance to the functioning of our daily lives. The course is particularly suited to my interests as I would have the opportunity to specialise in development economics and I would enjoy the academic rigour of applying maths to the analysis of economics. Furthermore, I would be able to draw from my other interests such as politics and history to augment my study of economics. I have started to use SPSS (statistical package for the social sciences) software in order to enhance my theoretical understanding of econometrics and because I enjoy using quantitative methods.

I find the collegiate nature of the university attractive because I love talking about the subject, and nothing is as enjoyable as to share one's interest with others who feel the same way about it! Also, as someone who values perspective, I think that discussing issues with people from different disciplines would facilitate the exchange of ideas and present new angles from which to address points of interest. I am also excited at the opportunity to discuss ideas in supervisions with people who are at the forefront of their field and who are engaged in active research.

Here's another example written by a modern languages applicant.

I am looking forward with confidence and enthusiasm to the challenge of completing French A level in the coming year before embarking on a modern languages degree course. Cambridge's emphasis on literature mirrors my own enthusiasm for French and Italian literature, and I was particularly thrilled to note that several lecturers have expertise in the works of Primo Levi, for whom I have great admiration, and who I would love to study at a higher level. As I am thinking of becoming a teacher, the idea of the year abroad greatly appeals, as it would give me valuable experience of teaching whilst improving my linguistic fluency.

Oxford no longer requires an additional form, with the three exceptions of: candidates for choral or organ awards, candidates wishing to be interviewed overseas, and graduate applicants for the Accelerated Medical Course. Some of the information which the Cambridge SAQ requires is collected in Oxford's case from the government's public information service. The information that the university will look at is as follows:

- the performance of your school or college at GCSE and A level or their equivalents, both using DfE or equivalent data (in both instances a candidate will be flagged if their educational establishment performs below the national average)
- the postcode of your home, assessed using Acorn information
- whether you have been looked after/in care for more than three months (determined from the UCAS application)
- whether you have participated in either a Sutton Trust summer school or the Oxford Young Ambassador Scheme.

Submitting written work

Another way admissions tutors decide whether or not to interview you – if you are applying for an essay-based subject – is by looking at a sample of your written work. This is something that you need to consider once you have submitted your application form(s). By looking at one of your essays, the admissions tutors will be able to assess your ability to research, organise information, form opinions, and construct a coherent and cogent argument in writing. These are essential skills to have when studying an essay subject at Oxbridge, and the admissions tutors need to see that you have these skills, and the potential to improve.

Normally the essay that you send will have been written as part of your A level course. Make sure that you send a particularly good example of your work; ask your teachers to suggest changes and then to re-mark the essay when you have improved it as much as possible. Do not, however, submit anything that could not have been written by you.

Plagiarism will be very obvious to admissions tutors and could potentially get you into some tricky situations at interview since submitted written work is often discussed at interview.

> 'The submitted essay is often used as the starting point for discussion in the interview. The essay can show us whether the candidate has the ability to argue and has academic confidence.'
> Admissions Tutor, Cambridge

The Oxford prospectus gives clear instructions about what you need to send and when. Remember to inform your teachers in advance that you will need to send marked work.

At Cambridge each college has a different policy on written work, but you are more likely to be asked to send in work if you are applying to read an arts or social sciences subject. The college will contact you directly if they require work from you.

If you have applied to Oxford, you will need to submit marked work for the following subjects:

- archaeology and anthropology
- classical archaeology and ancient history
- classics
- classics and English
- classics and modern languages
- classics and oriental studies
- computer science
- economics and management
- English and modern languages
- English language and literature
- European and Middle Eastern languages
- experimental psychology
- fine art
- geography
- history
- history (ancient and modern)
- history and economics
- history and English
- history and modern languages
- history and politics
- history of art
- law (jurisprudence) and law with law studies in Europe
- mathematics
- mathematics and computer science
- mathematics and philosophy
- mathematics and statistics
- medicine
- modern languages
- modern languages and linguistics
- music
- oriental studies
- philosophy and modern languages
- philosophy and theology
- physics
- physics and philosophy
- physiological sciences
- PPE
- PPP
- theology.

8 | Written tests

As more and more students are achieving A grades at A level, both Oxford and Cambridge are increasingly relying on other testing systems when selecting candidates for interview. These tests include the BMAT for medicine and the LNAT for law at Oxford: two externally administered tests. The HAT is sat for history at Oxford and there are various similar but internal exams set by Cambridge colleges. STEP papers have been reintroduced for maths at Cambridge as well as the TSA for various other Cambridge subjects. Not only do these exams aim to highlight the best students when A levels seem to be failing to do so, they also aim to widen access. Since it is often difficult to revise for the Oxbridge written tests, students have to rely on their innate intellectual creativity to complete them. In this way poorly schooled children are at no disadvantage.

The style of testing also differs from what many school leavers will be used to. Whereas A levels often test factual recall, the Oxbridge written exams look for analytical and critical capabilities. It should be noted, therefore, that these tests are likely to be much harder than anything you will have experienced at school. This is taken into consideration, and admissions tutors do not expect students to achieve 100%.

Oxford and Cambridge take quite different approaches to additional written tests. Oxford exams are standardised: for example, all students applying for history across the whole university will take exactly the same test (the HAT). In comparison, Cambridge tests vary from college to college: history applicants to Trinity, Girton, and Clare College might be set three completely different questions.

Testing happens at various stages during the application process. Some tests are sat in early November at your school (the BMAT, LNAT, and ELAT, for example). The results of these tests can then play a large part in determining whether you are called to interview. Some tests – including the majority of those for Cambridge – take place when you go up for interview in early December. The results are then used, alongside your interview performance, to decide whether you should be made a conditional offer.

The following chapter aims to give an account of the various written tests students face prior to or during their interviews, including: the deadlines for registering for the exams; when and where the tests are sat; details about the structure of the tests, including knowledge requirements; sample questions; and useful links for more information and practice.

Tables 3 and 4 explain which subjects require additional written tests at Oxford and Cambridge respectively. However, it is a good idea to check this information by ringing the admissions tutor at your college directly (see the college or university prospectus for the telephone number) or by going to the web addresses below.

- Cambridge: www.cam.ac.uk/admissions/undergraduate/courses
- Oxford: www.admissions.ox.ac.uk/interviews/tests

Table 3: Subjects tested at Oxford before the interview

Subject	Test
Economics and Management	TSA (Thinking Skills Assessment)
English	ELAT (English Literature Aptitude Test)
Experimental psychology	TSA (Specialist version)
History	HAT (History Aptitude Test)
Law	LNAT (The National Admissions Test for Law)
Maths (and all joint degrees/degrees where maths is a component)	Aptitude test for maths
Medicine and physiological sciences	BMAT (BioMedical Aptitude Test)
Physics (and all joint degrees including physics)	Physics Aptitude Test
PPE	TSA (Specialist version)
PPP	TSA (Specialist version)

Table 4: Subjects tested at Cambridge before the interview

Subject	Test
Computer science, economics, engineering, land economy, natural sciences, and social and political science (SPS)	TSA (used by some colleges)
Maths	STEP (Sixth Term Examination Papers – used by almost all colleges)
Medicine and veterinary medicine	BMAT (BioMedical Admissions Test)

BMAT (BioMedical Admissions Test), Oxford and Cambridge

For applications to medicine, physiological sciences (Oxford), and veterinary medicine (Cambridge):

- register online by the last week in September with a fee of £32.10 (waiveable)
- sit the BMAT in the first week of November at your school
- go to www.bmat.org.uk/faqstudent.html#gen15 for more information.

Both Oxford and Cambridge require students applying for medical school and for veterinary science to sit the BMAT exam. It aims to predict your potential as a medical student.

Structure: it is a two-hour paper that is sat at your school and there are three sections:

1. aptitude and skills (60 minutes, multiple choice)
2. scientific knowledge and applications (30 minutes, multiple choice)
3. essay writing task (30 minutes).

The BMAT requires GCSE-level knowledge of maths and GCSE Dual Science Award knowledge of biology, chemistry, and physics. The exam is structured so that biology, chemistry, and physics are equally weighted and maths is slightly less important.

Oxford and Cambridge will look at the scores of each section individually. Cambridge admissions tutors believe that Sections 1 and 2 correlate best with Tripos performance and therefore put an emphasis on these sections.

Perhaps the most important thing to prepare for with the BMAT is timing. There is relatively little time to get through a vast number of questions. You need to know the relevant A level and GCSE courses like the back of your hand so that you can apply your knowledge to complex situations without having to stop and think.

BMAT sample questions

BMAT section 1 question 7

The speed limit on motorways in the UK should be raised from 70mph to 80mph. The majority of drivers consistently break the current speed limit – and without penalty, as the police are unable to enforce the speed limit in all cases. There is no evidence to suggest that driving at 80mph is more dangerous than driving at 70mph. If the speed limit were raised, the police could devote more time to dealing with other crimes.

Which **one** of the following, if true, most weakens the above argument?

> **A** Many drivers choose to drive at below 70mph.
> **B** Modern cars are capable of speeds far in excess of 80mph.
> **C** Driving at 80mph uses more fuel than driving at 70mph.
> **D** With a speed limit of 80mph, more drivers would drive between 80mph and 90mph.
>
> Answer at the end of this chapter.
>
> *Section 3 – writing task (30 minutes)*
>
> **It is ridiculous to treat the living body as a mechanism.**
>
> Write a unified essay in which you address the following.
>
> What does the above statement imply?
>
> Give examples that illustrate why it might sometimes be sensible to treat the body as a mechanism and others that illustrate the opposite.
>
> How might you resolve this apparent contradiction?
>
> Source: From the specimen papers available on the Cambridge Assessment website www.admissionstests.cambridgeassessment.org.uk. Reprinted by permission of the University of Cambridge Local Examinations Syndicate.

ELAT (English Literature Aptitude Test), Oxford only

- Register online by mid-October.
- Sit ELAT in the first week of November at your school.
- Go to www.elat.org.uk for more information.

The ELAT tests the ability to read unfamiliar texts closely and to construct a focused essay.

Structure: the ELAT lasts for 90 minutes. You will be given six poems or prose passages and will be asked compare and contrast two or three of them. All six passages will be linked in some way and this will be made clear in the question. Your score will be placed into one of four bands, and those whose scores lie in the top two bands are the most likely to be called for interview.

ELAT sample question

The following poems and extracts from longer texts present views of fathers, mainly as seen by their children. Read all the material carefully, and then complete the task below.

(a) An extract from a novel by Philip Roth, *The Human Stain*, published in 2001.

(b) *To the Reverend Shade of His Religious Father*, a poem by Robert Herrick (1591–1674).

(c) An extract from a novel by Samuel Richardson, *Clarissa*, 1740, vol 1, Letter VIII. The novel is written entirely as a sequence of letters.

(d) *Carousel*, a poem by Lucinda Roy; first published in 1988.

(e) *Father's Bedroom*, a poem by Robert Lowell (1917–1977).

(f) An extract from a short story, *Grocer's Daughter*, by Marianne Wiggins, published in 1987.

Task

Select two or three of the passages (a) to (f) and compare and contrast them in any ways that seem interesting to you, paying particular attention to distinctive features of structure, language and style. In your introduction, indicate briefly what you intend to explore or illustrate through close reading of your chosen passages.

This task is designed to assess your responsiveness to unfamiliar literary material and your skills in close reading. Marks are not awarded for references to other texts or authors you have studied.

Source: From the specimen papers available on the Cambridge Assessment website www.admissionstests.cambridgeassessment.org.uk. Reprinted by permission of the University of Cambridge Local Examinations Syndicate.

HAT (History Aptitude Test), Oxford only

- Register online by mid-October.
- Sit the HAT in the first week of November at your school.
- Go to www.history.ox.ac.uk/prosundergrad/applying/hat_introduction.htm for more information.

The HAT will require you to discuss one of the historical periods you have studied at A level, so revision is essential. Oxford will automatically send the HAT results to your school. In general, the people who score in the bottom 20% of the HAT will be deselected.

The HAT tests the following skills and attributes:

- the ability to read carefully and critically
- the adoption of an analytical approach
- the ability to answer a question relevantly
- the ability to offer a coherent argument
- precision in the handling of concepts and in the selection of evidence presented to support points
- historical imagination
- originality
- precision, clarity, and facility of writing.

Make sure, when writing about a subject that you know well, to keep tightly to your plan, and not to get carried away displaying your knowledge. For the HAT, structure is incredibly important.

Structure of the test

The HAT website states:

> 'The HAT lasts for two hours and has two elements: a series of questions, including a short essay, based on a short piece of historical writing; and a single question, based on a primary source. Candidates are advised to spend about 40 minutes on reading the texts, thinking about them and planning their answers. The rest of the time they should spend on writing. Guidance is given about the form and length of each answer.'
>
> www.history.ox.ac.uk/prosundergrad/applying/
> hat_introduction.htm.

Section One (75–80 minutes, including reading, thinking and planning time). This section comprises three questions and is worth 70/100 marks:

1. **Definition exercise.** Understanding and defining terms drawn from the text. Relates to: careful and critical reading; precision in the handling of concepts; precision, clarity, and facility of writing. (10/100 marks)
2. **Explanation exercise.** Analysing and explaining terms drawn from the text. Relates to: careful and critical reading; analytical approach; precision in the handling of concepts; precision, clarity, and facility of writing. (20/100 marks)
3. **Essay exercise.** Applying a concept/hypothesis from the text to a historical situation; writing cogently at length. Relates to: analytical approach; coherent argument; precision in the handling of concepts and selection of evidence; relevance to the question; historical imagination; originality; precision, clarity, and facility of writing. (40/100 marks)

Section Two (40–45 minutes, including reading, thinking and planning time). This section comprises one question and is worth 30/100 marks:

1. **Interpretation exercise.** Interpretative response to primary source. Relates to: careful and critical reading; historical imagination; originality; precision, clarity and facility of writing.

> *Information taken from the Oxford undergraduate prospectus online: www.history.ox.ac.uk/prosundergrad/ applying/hat_introduction.htm.*

HAT example question

Oxford Colleges' History Aptitude Test, 4 November 2009

Question 2

This is an extract from a history of St Alban's Abbey, written by Thomas of Walsingham, a monk there in the 1390s.

> *Abbot Hugh (1339–49) 'caused a new crucifix to be made for the monastery church, whereupon the sculptor carved no specially beautiful or important feature except upon holy days only on which days he himself fasted on bread and water.*
>
> *'Moreover he had a naked man before him to look at, that he might learn from his form and carve the crucifix all the fairer. When this crucifix was set up, the Almighty constantly wrought many solemn and manifest miracles through it; wherefore we thought that if women might have access to the crucifix, the common devotion would be increased, and it would bring great profit to our monastery from gifts . . . (it was agreed) to admit men and women of good repute to the crucifix, provided only that the women should not enter through our cloister or dormitory or other domestic buildings, excepting only our patroness, or the wife or daughter of our patron; yet even these might not spend the night within the abbey precincts nor enter before Prime nor stay beyond Compline' . . . (In consequence) 'Women now flock frequently to the crucifix yet only to our own damage, since their devotion is but cold, and they only come to gaze at our church, and increase our expenses by claiming hospitality.'*

> What does this passage tell us about religious ideas, gender relations, and social structure in the fourteenth century?
>
> Source: This question is taken from the HAT paper for 2009 www.history.ox. ac.uk/prosundergrad/applying/documents/HAT_paper_2009.pdf. This and all other HAT papers can be accessed at: www.history.ox.ac.uk/prosundergrad/applying/hat_introduction.htm.

LNAT (The National Admissions Test for Law), Oxford only

- Register online by mid-October and pay £40 (waiveable).
- Sit the test from early September and before 1 November at a special test centre.
- Go to www.lnat.ac.uk for more information.

The first part of the LNAT – a multiple-choice section – is machine-marked and the results are passed in numerical form to the university that participates in the LNAT selection process. You will only receive your marks after the admissions process is over. The second part of the LNAT, an essay section, is passed unmarked to LNAT-participating universities.

Structure: the LNAT is a two-hour test and has two parts: a multiple-choice element (80 minutes) and an essay element (40 minutes).

The multiple-choice element consists of 10 argumentative passages, with three multiple-choice questions on each, making 30 questions in all. The questions are designed to test powers of comprehension, interpretation, analysis, synthesis, induction, and deduction. These are the verbal reasoning skills at the heart of legal education. The questions do not test (and do not require) knowledge of any subject except for the English language.

> 'The essay element gives you a choice of questions on a range of subjects. Although these typically require some rudimentary knowledge of everyday subjects, the point is not to test that knowledge but your ability to argue economically to a conclusion with a good command of written English. This part of the test is not centrally assessed.'
>
> Information taken from the LNAT website: www.lnat.ac.uk/2009/introduction/test.html.

For practice questions and mark schemes go to the LNAT website: www.lnat.ac.uk.

Aptitude test for maths, Oxford only

For applications to maths, maths with computer science, philosophy, statistics, or computer sciences:

- sit the test at your school at the end of October or beginning of November
- your school will be sent the papers automatically
- go to www.maths.ox.ac.uk/prospective-students/undergraduate/specimen-tests to see the syllabus for the exam and specimen papers.

Testing for maths and sciences at Oxford (and Cambridge) is largely based upon AS level knowledge. It is often the case, however, that relatively simple facts and formulas must be remembered in order to apply them to more complex and novel contexts. In this way, students must be able think 'outside the box' creatively. The test is set with the aim of being approachable by all students, including those without a Further Mathematics A level, and those from other educational systems (e.g. Baccalaureate and Scottish Highers). It aims to test the depth of student's mathematical understanding in the fourth term of their A levels (or equivalent) rather than a breadth of knowledge.

It is crucial that you do well in this paper since Oxford offers interviews based on student's success in the Aptitude Test.

Applicants will be shortlisted on the basis of the test score, together with information from their UCAS forms, and those shortlisted, in the UK and Europe, will be invited to Oxford in mid-December for interview.

Structure: the test lasts two and a half hours and there are seven questions in total. The first question is multiple choice and contains 10 parts, each worth four marks. Marks are given solely for the correct answers, although applicants are encouraged to show any working in the space provided. Questions 2–7 are longer questions, each worth 15 marks, and candidates will need to show their working. Candidates should attempt four questions from 2–7, the selection depending on the degree for which they are applying. Details of precisely which questions you should attempt are given in the rubric on the front page of the test and throughout the paper.

- *'No calculators, formula sheets, or dictionaries are permitted during the test.*
- *Only answers written in the booklet will be marked. There are spare blank pages at the end of the test paper.*

- *Further credit cannot be gained by attempting questions other than those appropriate to the degree applied for.'*

> *Information taken from Oxford Mathematics faculty website: www.maths.ox.ac.uk/prospective-students/ undergraduate/specimen-tests*

You should attempt some of the specimen/past tests provided on the website, so that you develop a sense of the format and style of the test, but no further preparation or practice, beyond work for A levels, is needed. Whilst two of the tests provided on the site are specimens, almost all the questions included were set on previous years' entrance tests.

Physics Aptitude Test, Oxford only

For applications to physics or physics and philosophy:

- test papers are automatically sent to your school
- sit the test in the first week of November at your school
- go to www.physics.ox.ac.uk/contact/ for more information on the physics department at Oxford.

There are two separate syllabuses: one for physics and another for maths for physics (A and B). Following is an outline of both. Oxford makes clear that the great majority of the knowledge required for this test will be familiar from GCSE and AS level mathematics and physics and that shortlisting for interview is largely based on the results of this aptitude test.

Syllabus for Part A of the aptitude test (mathematics for physics)

- **Elementary mathematics:** knowledge of elementary mathematics, in particular topics in arithmetic, geometry, including coordinate geometry, and probability, will be assumed.
- **Algebra:** properties of polynomials, including the solution of quadratics; graph sketching and transformations of variables; inequalities and their solution; elementary trigonometry, including relationships between sin, cos, and tan (sum and difference formulae will be stated if required); properties of logarithms and exponentials; arithmetic and geometric progressions and the binomial expansion.
- **Calculus:** differentiation and integration of polynomials including fractional and negative powers (but not integration of $1/x$); differentiation as finding the slope of a curve, and the location of maxima, minima, and points of inflection; integration as the reverse of differ-

entiation and as finding the area under a curve; simplifying integrals by symmetry arguments.

- **Physics:** knowledge of elementary physics will be assumed; questions may require the manipulation of mathematical expressions in a physical context.

Candidates who have studied mathematics at GCSE and AS level (including the first two core pure modules) should be familiar with the great majority of the syllabus.

Syllabus for Part B of the aptitude test (physics)

- **Mechanics:** distance, velocity, speed, acceleration, and the relationships between them; interpretation of graphs; response to forces (Newton's laws of motion; weight and mass; addition of forces; circular motion); friction, air resistance, and terminal velocity; levers, pulleys, and other elementary machines; springs and Hooke's law; kinetic and potential energy and their inter-conversion; other forms of energy; conservation of energy; power and work.
- **Waves and optics:** longitudinal and transverse waves; amplitude, frequency, period, wavelength and speed, and the relationships between them; basic properties of the electromagnetic spectrum; reflection at plane mirrors; refraction and elementary properties of prisms and lenses including total internal reflection (mathematical treatment not required); elementary understanding of interference and diffraction (mathematical treatment not required).
- **Electricity and magnetism:** current, voltage (potential difference), charge, resistance; relationships between them and links to energy and power; elementary circuits including batteries, wires, resistors, filament lamps, diodes, capacitors, light-dependent resistors and thermistors; series and parallel circuits; elementary electrostatic forces and magnetism (mathematical treatment not required); links between electricity and magnetism; electromagnets, motors, generators and transformers; current as a flow of electrons; thermionic emission and energy of accelerated electron beams.
- **The natural world:** atomic and nuclear structure; properties of alpha, beta, and gamma radiation; half lives; nuclear fission; structure of the solar system; phases of the moon and eclipses; elementary treatment of circular orbits under gravity including orbital speed, radius, period, centripetal acceleration, and gravitational centripetal force; satellites; geostationary and polar orbits; elementary properties of solids, liquids and gases including responses to pressure and temperature.
- **Mathematics:** knowledge of elementary mathematics will be assumed; questions may require the manipulation of mathematical expressions in a physical context.

- **Problem solving:** problems may be set which require problem solving based on information provided rather than knowledge about a topic.

Candidates who have studied physics at Higher Tier GCSE or AS level should be familiar with the great majority of the syllabus (www.physics. ox.ac.uk/admissions/syllabus.htm).

TSA (Thinking Skills Assessment), Oxford and Cambridge

For applicants to Cambridge to read: computer science, economics, engineering, natural sciences, land economy, philosophy and PPS. For applications to Oxford to read: economics and management, PPE, experimental psychology and computer science.

- Register by mid-October online.
- Sit the test at your school in the first week of November.
- Go to www.admissionstests.cambridgeassessment.org.uk for more information and specimen papers.

This test aims to measure your critical thinking and problem-solving skills, and is used to decide whether you should be asked to interview.

Structure: the TSA is a 90-minute multiple choice test consisting of 50 questions. There are two types of question in the test:

1. The problem-solving category is concerned with numerical and spatial reasoning (both understanding arguments and reasoning using everyday language). You may be asked to sift through information to identify important points or to compare or match argument structures.
2. The critical-thinking questions can involve the following:
   - summarising the main point
   - identifying an assumption
   - drawing a conclusion
   - identifying flaws in an argument
   - understanding the structure of an argument
   - applying principles.

Each question is worth one mark.

TSA sample questions

Cambridge TSA section 1 question 5

Some employers operate a three-shift system. This requires that, in any three-week period, an individual worker will have to work, for example, from 6am to 2pm in the first week, from 2pm to 10pm in the second week, and from 10pm to 6am in the third week. It becomes very difficult to establish any kind of routine of eating and drinking under such a system. People working a three-shift system report a severe decline in their appetite, especially during the night-shift when they would normally be asleep. Therefore anyone about to begin working shifts like this can expect to lose weight.

Which one of the following is an underlying assumption of the above argument?

A All shift workers have to work during the night.
B Employees tend to dislike working shifts.
C People who feel less hungry generally eat less food.
D Shift work often pays better than working days only.
E Canteen facilities are not always available to the night shift.

Answer at the end of the chapter.

Source: From the specimen papers available on the Cambridge Assessment website (www.admissionstests.cambridgeassessment.org.uk). Reprinted by permission of the University of Cambridge Local Examinations Syndicate.

Oxford TSA SECTION 2 QUESTION 4

Why is vision so important to human beings?

Source: From the specimen papers available on the Cambridge Assessment website (www.admissionstests.cambridgeassessment.org.uk). Reprinted by permission of the University of Cambridge Local Examinations Syndicate.

STEP (Sixth Term Examination Papers), Cambridge only

For applications to study mathematics and mathematics with physics, engineering, and computer science.

- The exam is taken in June at your school at the same time as your A levels.
- Your school must contact the Admissions Testing office at Cambridge (01223 558455) to request the STEP papers.

- Go to www.maths.cam.ac.uk/undergrad/admissions/step for more information.

Cambridge normally asks for STEPs as part of a conditional offer for maths and sometimes for the other subjects mentioned above. Whereas A level exam papers cannot be seen by universities, Cambridge admissions tutors can look at your STEP answer papers, thereby identifying your strengths and weaknesses more accurately. It is also important to realise that these exams are harder than A levels, and to adjust your expectations accordingly:

> 'STEP is supposed to be difficult: it is aimed at the top 5% or so of all A level mathematics candidates. It is therefore important to adjust your sights when tackling a STEP paper. The questions are much longer and more demanding than A level questions (they are intended to take about 45 minutes, rather than the 10 or so minutes for an A level question). They therefore look daunting; but you should not be daunted. In recent years, you only had to give good (not perfect) answers to four questions for a grade 1.'
>
> Information taken from the Cambridge website:
> www.maths.cam.ac.uk/undergrad/admissions/step

Structure: there are three STEP mathematics papers, numbered I, II, and III. Your offer will usually include grades in two of the papers, normally I and II if you are not taking the full Further Mathematics A level (or an equivalent qualification), or II and III if you are taking Further Mathematics A level (or an equivalent qualification).

Each paper consists of 13 questions: eight pure, three mechanics, and two statistics and probability. Each paper is assessed on answers to at most six questions. There are five grades, which are (from highest to lowest) S, 1, 2, 3, and U.

> 'The syllabus for Mathematics I and II is based on a typical single subject A level syllabus: the Pure Mathematics content is very slightly more than the A level common core. The syllabuses for the Mechanics and the Probability and Statistics sections are each equivalent to two or three A level modules but, since there is no common core for these areas, the material may not coincide with the modules of your particular A level. Paper I is intended specifically for candidates who are not taking Further Mathematics (or the equivalent) and the questions are intended to be easier than those in Paper II. The syllabus for Mathematics III is based on a typical Further Mathematics A level syllabus (there is no Further Mathematics core syllabus) and the questions are intended to be of about the same level of difficulty as those of Paper II.'
>
> Information taken from the Cambridge website:
> www.maths.cam.ac.uk/undergrad/admissions/step

The best way to prepare is to work through past exam papers. The following example will give you an idea of the sorts of questions you may be asked.

STEP 2010 paper iii *Section B: Mechanics*

Question 11

A bullet of mass m is fired horizontally with speed u into a wooden block of mass M at rest on a horizontal surface. The coefficient of friction between the block and the surface is   . While the bullet is moving through the block, it experiences a constant force of resistance to its motion of magnitude R, where $R > (M + m)$ g. The bullet moves horizontally in the block and does not emerge from the other side of the block.

(i)   Show that the magnitude, a, of the deceleration of the bullet relative to the block while the bullet is moving through the block is given by:

$$a = \frac{R}{m} + \frac{R - (M + m) \ g}{M}.$$

(ii) Show that the common speed, v, of the block and bullet when the bullet stops moving through the block satisfies:

$$av = \frac{Ru - (M + m) \ gu}{M}.$$

(iii) Obtain an expression, in terms of u, v and a, for the distance moved by the block while the bullet is moving through the block.

(iv) Show that the total distance moved by the block is:

$$\frac{muv}{2 (M + m) \ g}.$$

Describe briefly what happens if $R < (M + m)$ g.

Source: From the specimen papers available on the Cambridge Assessment website (www.admissionstests.cambridgeassessment.org.uk). Reprinted by permission of the University of Cambridge Local Examinations Syndicate.

Useful links and resources for mathematics test preparation.

- **STEP Specification:** this can be found on the CA website (www.stepmathematics.org.uk) and at the end of the Advanced Problems in the Core Mathematics booklet.
- **Advanced Problems in Core Mathematics:** (www.maths.cam.ac.uk/undergrad/admissions/step/advpcm.pdf): a booklet by Stephen Siklos, containing general advice on problem solving accompanied by 70 or so problems with hints and full solutions, and the STEP syllabuses. This would be a good starting point for your preparation.
- **AskNRICH:** (www.nrich.maths.org/askedNRICH/edited/menu/step.html) collated answers to STEP-related questions fielded by the AskNRICH project.
- **Miekleriggs Mathematics:** (www.meikleriggs.org.uk) Dr Peter Mitchell's website contains lots of useful mathematics including complete solutions to STEP papers from past years.
- **Stephen Siklos's website:** (www.damtp.cam.ac.uk/user/stcs) this contains some additional material, including a few video solutions of STEP questions.
- **Advanced Problems in Mathematics:** this booklet by Stephen Siklos consists of 43 STEP-like problems with discussion, hints and full solutions. It is available, at modest price, from OCR publications. But beware: it was written before the current syllabuses were in place.

For more information or help booking your test you can also email the Cambridge Assessment help line: stepinfo@cambridgeassessment.org.uk; or ring the help desk: 01223 558455.

Tests for modern languages, Oxford and Cambridge

- Normally taken when you go up for interview.
- Specimens for tests at Oxford: www.ox.ac.uk/admissions/undergraduate_courses/how_to_apply/tests/index.html
- Specimens for Cambridge tests: www.cam.ac.uk/admissions/undergraduate/apply/tests.html

The modern languages courses at Oxford and Cambridge place emphasis on different aspects of language. The Cambridge course focuses on literature and culture, Oxford on grammar and linguistics. The tests taken just before interview at the universities reflect these differences. You will not be expected to have practised this type of test before, and will be at no disadvantage if you have not. The Cambridge admissions website is keen to reassure you:

'The test forms just one small part of the overall assessment of applicants (based on your written application, your school/college record, interviews, etc.): even if you do not do particularly well at this written test, it is perfectly possible for you still to be offered a place.'
www.mml.cam.ac.uk/prospectus/undergrad/test.html

The structure is as follows.

- The Oxford test is usually a 30-minute-long test and is divided into two sections. The first asks you to analyse the grammar of short sentences in your chosen language. The second section is a short translation from the target language that you wish to study at university back into English.
- At Cambridge, you will be given 45 minutes to read a brief passage in English (300–350 words) and then asked to answer two or three questions about it.

'You will write your answer in the target language that you are studying at A level (A2) or equivalent and for which you are applying to study at Cambridge University. The questions will contain an element of comprehension but will also invite you to add ideas of your own. In other words, the exercise is a combination of comprehension and free composition. The purpose is to see how you write in the foreign language: i.e. it assesses your grammar, accuracy, ability to express ideas, and vocabulary, though you are not expected to know the exact foreign-language term for each English term in the passage.'
www.mml.cam.ac.uk/prospectus/undergrad/test.html

Non-standardised tests at Cambridge (during interview)

Although testing at Cambridge is less standardised, the exams tend to be similar in content to those Oxford exams mentioned earlier in this chapter. It is advisable, for example, to practise HAT papers even if you are applying to read history at Cambridge. The same is true for English: questions will probably be comparable to the ELAT.

General preparation for logic-based tests

To look at past papers and mark schemes for the critical-thinking GCSEs, A levels and AEA that the exam boards AQA and OCR set, go to:

- http://web.aqa.org.uk/qual/gce/humanities/critical_thinking_overview.php
- www.ocr.org.uk/qualifications/type/gce/hss/critical_thinking/faqs/index.html

For questions similar to the critical thinking components of BMAT, ELAT, HAT, LNAT, and TSA, go to:

- www.shl.com/TryATest/Pages/CandidateHelp.aspx
- www.shldirect.com/example_questions.html

Note that these websites link to graduate recruitment sites and will be particularly challenging.

Further reading

Bryon, Mike, *Critical Thinking and Problem Solving*. London: Kogan Page, 2006 (the ultimate psychometric test book).

Fisher, A., *Critical Thinking: An Introduction*. Cambridge: CUP, 2001.

Hodges, Willfred, *Logic*, 2nd revised edition. London: Penguin, 2001.

Martin, Robert, *There are Two Errors in the the Title of This Book: A Source Book of Philosophical Puzzles, Paradoxes and Problem*. Canada: Broadview Press, 1992.

Rhodes, Peter, *Practice Tests for Critical Verbal Reasoning: Succeed at Psychometric Testing*. London: Hodder Arnold, 2006.

Sainsbury, Mark, *Logical Forms*, 2nd revised edition. Hoboken, NJ: Wiley Blackwell, 2000.

Shavick, Andrea, *Management Level Psychometric and Assessment Tests*. Oxford: How To Books, 2005.

Taylor, F., Hutton R. and Hutton, G., *Passing the UK Clinical Aptitude Test (UKCAT) and BMAT*, 2nd revised edition. Exeter: Learning Matters Publishing, 2007.

Answers

BMAT: Whilst options **A, B** and **C** might be true, they are of little relevance to the argument.

The suggested benefit of raising the limit (that less police time would be spent enforcing the speed limit) would be reduced if more drivers drove at over 80mph and so continued to break the speed limit. The correct answer is **D**.

Cambridge TSA: Answer: **C**.

9 | The interview

Why are Oxford and Cambridge interviews important?

The interview happens in the first three weeks of December and is the single most important part of the selection process at Oxford and Cambridge. This is because this is the first point in the application process when you meet your potential tutors or supervisors. You may look great on paper – have a brilliant Personal Statement and faultless exam grades – but you must make a good impression at interview too in order to be selected. Oxford and Cambridge interview about 90% of the students who apply. This means that, if everything else has gone to plan so far, it is likely you will get the chance to impress the tutors at your chosen college in person. However, so will everyone else. The competition is still very high!

The number of applicants to places varies considerably depending on subject choice. For economics, for example, there are often five applicants interviewed for one place. For architecture at Cambridge there are 10 or more applicants interviewed for one place. These statistics are given in the prospectuses.

If you do get asked for interview, you will be sent a letter and email any time between mid-November and early December. This letter will give you the dates and times when you are required to arrive at your college and directions for how to get there. On arriving at Oxford or Cambridge you will normally go straight to your college: this is where you will be based for the duration of your stay. At this point you will get your interview timetable, a map of the university grounds and of the college.

If you need to stay overnight you will be given a room of your own and free food will be available at set times of day in college 'halls' (the canteen). There are often current undergraduates on hand to usher interviewees to the right place at the right time, so you can be sure that you will be made comfortable and welcome. Remember, the porters – stationed near the front entrance in the porter's lodge – love to be helpful; it's their job. If you have any questions about practical matters, or if you get lost, just head in their direction.

There are a number of key differences between Oxford and Cambridge in terms of their interview practice.

- Cambridge interviews normally span one day only, Oxford's between two and five.

- At Oxford it is possible to have interviews at other colleges during your stay, but first round interviews at Cambridge will take place at your college of choice only.
- Cambridge will tell you your interview date well in advance, Oxford will give you short notice and expect you to know when to arrive by the 'provisional date' section in the prospectus. Oxford reserves the right to call a candidate to interview any time up until a week before the provisional date given.
- Cambridge makes known individual interview start times and locations in advance, Oxford does not.
- Oxford will inform you of their decision before Christmas, Cambridge after.

There are no hard and fast rules about how interviews at Oxford and Cambridge are structured, or how many interviewers there will be in the room with you at one time. There may just be one interviewer; there may be a panel of two or more. Each interview normally lasts 30–45 minutes and takes place in a room – normally the office of your potential tutor or director of studies – in the college.

At Cambridge, candidates are often asked to attend two interviews over the period of one or two days: one is normally subject-specific, and the other is more general. Make sure you know which one you are walking into so that you can tailor your responses appropriately. It is not always obvious, so ask if you are uncertain.

At Oxford, students are normally asked to stay over a period of several days and nights at their chosen college and may need to attend as many as four or five subject-specific interviews across the university.

So what exactly are the interviewers looking for?

There are a few essential characteristics that interviewers will be looking for, some of which you will already have considered when writing your Personal Statement. These include:

1. **passion for your subject**
2. **knowledge of your subject** and a very good understanding of the school syllabus (if relevant)
3. the ability to think **critically and analytically**
4. the ability to think **independently**
5. **'teachability'** (the ability to listen and work well in a supervision setting).

Passion for your subject

Having a passion for your subject is possibly the most important thing to get across during an interview. To come this far you will already have had to prove that you are academically capable. However, it is your excitement about your chosen subject and an enthusiasm to learn more about it that will interest your interviewers. Remember, they will be dedicating their teaching time to you, possibly with an idea to training you up to join their faculty in years to come, and they take their work very seriously. Passion for your subject can be illustrated in a variety of ways.

- Your body language at the interview and the way you communicate with your interviewers: if you smile, talk energetically and enthusiastically, and look interested when they offer their ideas, this will give them the feeling that you are really passionate about the subject.
- If you have read a great deal and are ready to discuss what you have explored with your interviewer, you are obviously seriously interested in your chosen subject.
- If you have taken the time to organise work experience related to your subject and/or you have taken part in a variety of extracurricular activities, and you can discuss this with your interviewer, then you will show your commitment to your chosen field.

Knowledge of your subject

Knowledge about your subject is often important as a starting point for further study at university, particularly in science subjects.

If you have studied your subject at school, interviewers will expect you to know the syllabus inside out as a starting point for discussion, before pushing you further. Interviewers will find out about your knowledge in several ways.

- They may ask A level syllabus-related questions, such as: 'Which module did you enjoy most in biology this year?' Make the most of a question like this to really show the interviewer what you know. Rather than giving a one-word answer, elaborate and explain why. Go into as much detail as you can.
- In mathematics or science subjects, interviewers will probably give you practical questions to work out. These may start with problems that you have encountered before at school and then progress to harder ones.

Critical and analytical thinking

The ability to think critically and analytically is very important at university. Interviewers want to see that you can play with ideas and make judgements about what you have read/seen. This shows that you can form opinions of your own and are able to organise information coherently in your head, and then in words. Interviewers can test you on this in several ways.

- When interviewing for arts or humanities subjects, interviewers may ask you questions that specifically require you to make judgements and organise your ideas. For example, in an interview to read English they might ask: 'So, what do you think is particularly striking about the war poetry of Wilfred Owen?' A good candidate may perhaps discuss several poems, one by one, pointing out one idea per poem. This would be a narratival approach to the question and would prove that the candidate had good knowledge of the subject, but would not show that they could think critically about it. Better candidates will think about common themes that run through all Owen's war poetry and then consider which theme is the most 'striking'. This candidate would have critically analysed her/his ideas and organised the answer into a coherent argument.
- In terms of sciences, an interviewer might show you some data or a series of graphs and expect you to make sense of them, realising patterns and/or differences between groups of information. This would show that you can analyse and make sense of the information.

Independent thinking

It is also important to show that you can think independently and 'outside the box'. An ability to think around a question shows flair and initiative and is very attractive to interviewers. In all subjects studied at Oxbridge undergraduate students are expected to absorb incredible amounts of information through independent reading and research. It is therefore very important that you can think and work for yourself. To explore your independence, an interviewer may ask you about a subject which you have never come across before. Interviewers may ask different questions to assess your independence of mind, for example:

- in a mathematics interview, the interviewer may show you a new type of simultaneous equation. You may never have seen this type, but if you attempt to solve it by using the principles you have learnt when tackling simpler problems you will be using your knowledge creatively and independently
- similarly, in a science interview you might be taught some new information by an interviewer regarding a particular chemical reaction. The interviewer might then give you a question to solve alone. If you can use the information just taught to you to solve this new question then you will be illustrating your ability to think on your feet independently and creatively

- in a humanities subject, for example history, the interviewer could ask you to discuss the potential causes for an obscure event that you know little or nothing about. In this instance, if you can compare the event to one that you have studied, you may be able to apply your previous knowledge to the new situation. Rather than giving up, you would have shown intellectual courage and lateral thinking.

Teachability

Finally, it is very important that the interviewer feels like he or she can imagine teaching you in a small group on a regular basis. The interview set-up is quite similar to a seminar or tutorial so, if you are accepted, you and your interviewer will be working together like this every week. Much of what will make the interviewer feel comfortable has been said above. If you are passionate, independently minded, and have worked hard previously, your interviewer will probably feel you are a worthwhile candidate. However, if you fit with the following criteria, you are probably particularly suited to the tutorial system.

- You feel comfortable discussing your ideas out loud and are not shy to give your opinions.
- You are also someone who can listen carefully to suggestions, and are able to adapt your opinions in order to take the ideas of the tutors or supervisors on board.

Finally, when thinking about what admissions tutors find attractive, it may be useful to consider what they do not want to see. Admissions tutors have said that there are common mistakes or traits that unsuccessful applicants have. Unsuccessful applicants:

> 'are too eager to agree/not keen to discuss/debate
> are well informed but cautious or uncritical in thinking
> have difficulty when challenged to think for themselves
> are reluctant to engage with the unfamiliar
> jump into answers without listening.'
>
> *Admissions Tutor, Cambridge*

Interview styles

'If you could put four things into a space capsule and send it into outer space, what would you chose?'

I was asked this question during a history interview at Cambridge in 2002. I should have asked what my interviewer meant, and whether he could give me some more information, but I was too intimidated. Horror stories about unkind Oxbridge interviewers asking completely random questions abound. In the newspapers and by word of mouth we are told that we will be asked things that seem totally unrelated to the subject we hope to study. This is, however, uncommon, and I was unlucky. As an interviewer for history at Oxford says:

> 'This type of question should not be asked and rarely is. We do not want to trick you or to make you look stupid. We simply want to find out how your mind works. If you are asked a strange question, you are well within your rights to ask the interviewer what they mean or want.'
>
> Oxford Interviewer, 2009

What is clear, however, is that many interviewers do not have any formal training. They are academics, not employers. They are probably perfectly nice people but may not be excellent communicators. They are human and make mistakes and they can often phrase questions unclearly. If this happens you can ask them to clarify. They may rephrase the question for you, or they may decide not to and wait to see what you come up with. There are as many different interview styles as there are interviewers, but you can be prepared for some of the tougher ones just in case.

The passive interviewer

This type of interviewer can be the hardest to deal with. It doesn't matter how enthusiastic you are you just can't get them to seem interested in what you are saying. This can make you feel crushed and unsure about how well you are doing. The only thing you can do in this situation is to keep your head up and carry on going.

Alternatively, the interviewer may seem so laid back that anything you say is acceptable. This can be dangerous. Whereas a pushy interviewer will put pressure on you to find the right answer or develop your argument, the laid-back interviewers will not. They may either be happy with one-word answers from you, talking endlessly themselves, or they may let you rabbit away without giving you any direction. Either way, it is hard to show your full potential in this sort of situation. If this happens you need to be very aware of the length of your answers. Try to expand your responses so that you show the breadth of your knowledge but do not talk for too long. Your answers should never continue for more than one minute without input, however small, from your interviewer.

Don't be fooled by a passive or relaxed interviewer. Just because they are reclining in their chair does not mean you can lie back in yours. Remember, you are performing. Keep your mind clearly focused on the task at hand.

The aggressive interviewer

A brutal interview can be a terrifying experience and can make the most confident candidates quake in their seats. First of all, keep a clear head and never take anything personally. A good intellectual argument can be a very attractive thing to an academic. One of the common features of this interview style is the oft-repeated question 'And????'. Whatever you say, however you develop your argument, the interviewer exclaims, 'And?' at the end of your answer, before you have a chance to gasp for breath. When faced with this situation, keep thinking around the subject. You could say, 'Well, I am not sure, but you could look at it like this: . . .' or 'I guess an alternative angle might be . . .'. Keep going and keep thinking. If you have exhausted all the possibilities that you can think of, a good way to give in is: 'I really can't think of anything else, but I would love to find out. Could you tell me?' You will show that you are interested and this is a key factor in the make-up of a good candidate. The interviewer may well have a very specific answer in mind that you could not have possibly guessed. However, in these situations, the process is often more important than the solution. Remember, they want to find out how your mind works, not just what you know.

Aggressive interviewers may ask you obscure questions that seem to be intended purely to catch you out. At all times, especially when unsure about the question, verbalise your thought processes. It is always a good idea to stop and think for a few seconds before launching into an answer. Once you have thought about one point you could say: 'I haven't thought about this before, but it seems similar to . . .'. If you do not understand the question ask the interviewer to clarify. Be up-front and open.

An interviewer may also play devil's advocate and argue with you just for the sake of it. He or she will be testing your ability to formulate a strong argument and to stick by it. When discussing contentious issues, make sure not to generalise. Always think of some empirical data or detailed proof to back up your judgement. In this way you will strengthen your argument and make it harder for the interviewer to back you into a corner. In a heated discussion don't be afraid to follow through with your ideas to the end. Take care, however, if things get too heated, to back down gracefully. Your interviewer may have been working in his or her field since before you were born, and will know what they are talking about.

The scribbler

In some interviews there will be more than one interviewer. Often, in this situation, one person will talk and another will scribble down notes. It may be disconcerting watching someone 'marking' your performance in front of you, and you may feel unsure about whom to address your answers to. The best course of action is to ignore the second person as much as possible. Listen to the interviewer who speaks and then respond to him/her. Of course, include the other interviewer if he or she looks up, but don't feel you need to wait for a response from them before continuing with your discussion.

A positive note

Remember, the above styles are worst case scenarios. It is the interviewer's job to make you feel comfortable. If the experience feels odd, this may be just as much a reflection of your interviewer's style as your own performance. With luck, and a well-prepared and friendly interviewer, your experience should feel like an informal discussion about something you are very interested in, and will not feel intimidating at all.

General preparation

It is a very good idea to predict the questions you might be asked at interview and practise working through your responses. Here are some tips.

1. An obvious place to start is your **Personal Statement**. Your interviewers are likely to have this on the table in front of them during the interview and will have skimmed through it immediately before you arrive. This will be used as a starting point for discussion. They are likely to pick up on any books and articles you have mentioned or subjects you say you particularly enjoyed at school. Make sure you have re-read everything you mention in your Personal Statement and are ready to discuss your ideas.

2. **Get to know your interviewer before you arrive.** Before you arrive at the interview you might find it useful to find out a bit about your interviewer. As you will remember, an academic from the faculty of your choice will also be a 'fellow' of the college that you are applying to. You can check who this is either by looking at the relevant faculty website and reading the list of staff, or by going to the college website and doing the same thing. It is this 'fellow' who is likely to be your tutor or DOS and will probably be your interviewer. It is, therefore, a good idea to know where his/her particular interests lie. Although, at undergraduate level, your work will be faculty-based, it is always a bonus if the academic at the college that you are applying to has done research in an area you find fascinating. Your interviewer's research interests will be listed alongside their name on the faculty or college website. Don't try to read every book and article they have ever written. This will be impossible. Just

having looked them up, and perhaps mentioning your interest in their work, shows an independence and enthusiasm that will be appreciated. Knowing a little bit about who they are and what they are interested in will also make you feel more comfortable when you meet them.

3. **Be prepared to be given reading material.** Particularly in arts and humanities subjects, reading material is often given to interviewees an hour prior to a subject-specific interview. For history, for example, you may be given a primary source to analyse. For English, you may be given a poem or a short story to read. For geography you may be given a map or photograph to study. These tasks will form the first part of the interview and will give you a chance to prove how well you can think on your feet. In some cases interviewers will even give you additional tasks to do when you are in the room with them.

4. **Problem solving in science subjects and mathematics.** In interviews for science subjects and mathematics, a large part of any subject-specific interview will consist of working through problems in front of your interviewer. These will normally start simply and relate closely to your A level syllabus. They will then get progressively harder. Try to apply knowledge from situations you have encountered before to unfamiliar questions, and remember to verbalise your thought processes, particularly if you are stuck.

5. **Interviews in other languages.** If you are applying to read modern languages and have studied your chosen language to A level, the interviewer may conduct your discussions in that language. If you hope to study a language from scratch, for example Russian, you will not be expected to speak Russian to your interviewer. You may be given some comprehension, translation, or grammar work to do an hour prior to your subject-specific interview, and this will form the first part of your discussion.

6. **Questions about current affairs.** Be prepared to discuss current affairs that relate to your chosen subject. Keep up to date by reading newspapers, recent journal publications, and magazines in your field if you have access to them. Most things are easily available on the web. Listen to the radio and search for relevant blogs and podcasts.

For more information you should also go to the Oxford and Cambridge University websites and search for 'interview questions'. The Oxford site offers example interview questions in a range of subjects, with explanations from interviewers about what they are looking for in the answers. Both universities also have podcasts and video clips of interviews as well as admissions tutors discussing the admissions process. Looking at these will help you visualise your own interview and mentally prepare yourself for the experience. A few interview questions are listed overleaf to get you thinking.

General interview questions

- Why do you want to come to this college?
- What made you want to study this subject?
- What are you intending to do in your gap year?
- Where do you see yourself in five years' time?
- Excluding your A level reading, what were the last three books you read?
- What do you regard as your strengths and weaknesses?
- What extra-curricular activities would you like to take part in at this college?
- Why did you make an open application?
- Give us three reasons why we should offer you a place.
- What will you do if we don't?
- Why did you choose your A level subjects?
- How will this degree help in your chosen career?
- How would your friends describe you?

Subject-specific interview questions

Anthropology and archaeology

- Name the six major world religions.
- What does Stonehenge mean to you?
- What are the problems regarding objectivity in anthropological studies?
- Why do civilisations erect monuments?
- Why should we approach all subjects from a holistic, anthropological perspective?

Architecture

A large part of the interview is likely to be dedicated to discussing your portfolio. Be prepared to discuss the ideas, purposes, and motivations behind your work. Your work should also illustrate a well-developed ability to relate two- and three-dimensional experience through drawing and 3D models. You should also be prepared to discuss your work experience. Below are some other questions that might be included.

- Is architecture in decline?
- Could you describe a building that you recently found interesting?
- Do you have an architect whom you particularly admire? What is it about their work that you find attractive?
- If you could design a building anywhere in the world, and if money, space, and time were unlimited, what would you design?

Art history

- What do we look for when we study art? What are we trying to reveal?
- Comment on this painting on the wall.
- Compare and contrast these three images.
- What exhibitions have you been to recently?
- How do you determine the value of art?
- Who should own art?
- What is art?
- Why is art important?
- What role do art galleries and museums play in society today?
- Are humans inherently creative?
- Apart from your studies, how else might you pursue your interest in art history while at the university?
- What are some key themes in the history of art?
- How has the depiction of the human form developed through the centuries?
- Who invented linear perspective: artists or architects?
- When was the discipline of art history brought to England and by whom?

Biochemistry

- How do catalysts work?
- Describe the work of enzymes.
- Discuss the chemistry of the formation of proteins.
- Questions on oxidation, equilibria, and interatomic forces.
- Questions on X-ray crystallography.
- Why do you wish to read biochemistry rather than chemistry?
- What scientific journals have you read lately? Is there a recent development in the field that particularly interests you?
- Why does most biochemistry take place away from equilibrium? (Or: How important is equilibrium to biochemical processes?)

Biological sciences

- How does the immune system recognise invading pathogens as foreign cells?
- How does a cell stop itself from exploding due to osmosis?
- Why is carbon of such importance in living systems?
- How would you transfer a gene to a plant?
- Explain the mechanism of capillary action.
- What are the advantages of the human genome project?
- How would you locate a gene for a given characteristic in the nucleus of a cell?
- What is the major problem with heart transplants in the receiver?
- Should we be concerned about GMOs? Why or why not?
- Do cellular processes take place at equilibrium?

- How important are primary electrogenic pumps for transmembrane ion transport of organic molecules? Why are these important?
- Why do plants, fungi, and bacteria utilise H+ gradients to energise their membranes whereas animals utilise Na+ gradients?

Chemistry

- Questions on organic mechanisms.
- Questions on structure, bonding, and energetics.
- Questions on acids and bases.
- Questions on isomerisation.
- Questions on practical chemical analysis.
- Describe the properties of solvents and mechanisms of salvation.

(See also biochemistry questions.)

Classics

- Questions on classical civilisations and literature.
- Why do you think ancient history is important?
- How civilised was the Roman world?
- Apart from your A level texts, what have you read in the original or in translation?

Earth sciences and geology

- Where would you place this rock sample in geological time?
- How would you determine a rock's age?
- Can you integrate this decay curve, and why would the result be useful?
- Questions on chemistry.
- When do you think oil will run out?

Economics

- Explain how the Phillips curve arises.
- Would it be feasible to have an economy which was entirely based on the service sector?
- A man pays for his holiday at a hotel on a tropical island by cheque. He has a top credit rating and rather than cashing it, the hotelier pays a supplier using the same cheque. That supplier does the same thing with one of his suppliers and so on ad infinitum. Who pays for the man's holiday?
- What do you know about the interaction between fiscal and monetary policy?
- I notice that you study mathematics. Can you see how you might derive the profit maximisation formula from first principles?
- Tell me about competition in the television industry.
- How effective is current monetary policy?
- What are your particular interests as regards economics?

- Do you think we should worry about a balance of payments deficit?
- If you were the Chancellor of the Exchequer, how would you maximise tax revenue?
- If you had a fairy godmother who gave you unlimited sums of money, what sort of company would you start and what types of employee would you hire?
- What are the advantages and disadvantages of joining the eurozone?
- What are the qualities of a good economist?
- Why are you studying Economics A level?
- What would happen to employment and wage rates if the pound depreciated?
- Do you the think the Chinese exchange rate will increase?
- How does the housing market affect inflation?
- How has social mobility changed in recent times?
- How best can the government get us out of the recession?

Engineering

- Questions on mathematics and physics, particularly calculus and mechanics.
- Questions on mathematical derivations, for example, of laws of motion.
- Look at this mechanical system sitting on my desk: how does it work?
- How do aeroplanes fly?
- What is impedance matching and how can it be achieved?
- How do bicycle spokes work?
- How would you divide a tetrahedron into two identical parts?
- What is the total resistance of the tetrahedron if there are resistors of one ohm on each edge?
- How would you design a gravity dam for holding back water?

English

- Why might it be useful for English students to read the *Twilight* series?
- What do you consider to be the most important work of literature of the twentieth century?
- Who is your favourite author?
- Apart from your A level texts, what book have you read recently, and why did you enjoy it?
- Give a review of the last play you saw at the theatre.
- Critically analyse this poem.
- How has the author used language in this text?

Geography

- Is geography just a combination of other disciplines?
- If I were to visit the area in which you live, what would I find interesting?

- Why should geography be studied in its own right?
- Would anything remain of geography if we took the notion of place off the syllabus?
- How important is the history of towns when studying settlement patterns?
- Why is climate so unpredictable?
- What is the importance of space in global warming?
- Why do you think people care about human geography more than physical geography?
- What is more important, mapping or computer models?
- If you went to an isolated island to do research on the beach, how would you use the local community?
- Analyse a graph about a river. Why are there peaks and troughs?
- Look at a world map showing quality of life indicators. Explain the pattern in terms of two of the indicators.

(See also questions on land economy.)

History

- Discuss an historical movement that you find particularly interesting.
- How can one define revolution?
- Why did imperialism happen?
- Who was the greater democrat: Gladstone or Disraeli?
- Was the fall of the Weimar Republic inevitable?
- 'History is the study of the present with the benefit of hindsight.' Do you agree?
- Would history be worth studying if it didn't repeat itself?
- What is the difference between modern history and modern politics?
- What is the position of the individual in history?
- Would you abolish the monarchy for ideological or practical reasons?
- Why do historians differ in their views on Hitler?
- What skills should a historian have?
- In what periods has the Holy Grail been popular, with whom, and why?
- Why is it important to visit historical sites relevant to the period you are studying?

Human sciences

- Talk about bovine spongiform encephalopathy and its implications, and the role of prions in Creutzfeldt–Jakob disease.
- What causes altitude sickness and how do humans adapt physiologically to high altitudes?
- Tell me about the exploitation of indigenous populations by Westerners.
- Why is statistics a useful subject for human scientists?
- Why are humans so difficult to experiment with?

- How would you design an experiment to determine whether genetics or upbringing is more important?
- What are the scientific implications of globalisation on the world?

Land economy

- Will the UK lose its sovereignty if it joins the eurozone?
- Will the eurozone encourage regionalism?
- Will the information technology revolution gradually result in the death of inner cities?
- What has been the effect of the Channel Tunnel on surrounding land use?

Law

- Questions on the points of law arising from scenarios, often relating to criminal law or duty of care.
- What does it mean to 'take' another's car?
- A cyclist rides the wrong way down a one-way street and a chimney falls on him. What legal proceedings should he take? What if he is riding down a private drive signed 'no trespassing'?
- X intends to poison his wife but accidentally gives the lethal draught to her identical twin. Would you consider this a murder?
- Questions on legal issues, particularly current ones.
- Should stalking be a criminal offence?
- Should judges have a legislative role?
- Do you think that anyone should be able to serve on a jury?
- Should judges be elected?
- Do judges have political bias?
- To what extent do you think the press should be able to release information concerning allegations against someone?
- Who do you think has the right to decide about euthanasia?
- How does the definition of intent distinguish murder from manslaughter?
- Can you give definitions of murder and manslaughter?
- Should foresight of consequences be considered as intending such consequences?

Material sciences

- Questions on physics, particularly solid materials.
- Questions on mathematics, particularly forces.
- Investigations of sample materials, particularly structure and fractures.

Maths and computation

- Questions (which may become progressively harder) on almost any area of the A level syllabus.

Maths and further maths

- Pure maths questions on integration.
- Applied maths questions on forces.
- Statistics questions on probability.
- Computation questions on iterations, series, and computer arithmetic.

Medicine

- What did your work experience teach you about life as a doctor?
- What did you learn about asthma in your work experience on asthma research?
- How have doctors' lives changed in the past 30 years?
- Explain the logic behind the most recent NHS reforms.
- What are the mechanisms underlying diabetes?
- Why is it that cancer cells are more susceptible to destruction by radiation than normal cells?
- How would you determine whether leukaemia patients have contracted the disease owing to a nearby nuclear power station?
- What does isometric exercise mean in the context of muscle function?
- What can you tell me about the mechanisms underlying sensory adaptation?
- What is an ECG?
- Why might a general practitioner not prescribe antibiotics to a toddler?
- Why are people anxious before surgery? Is it justifiable?
- How do you deal with stress?
- Why does your heart rate increase when you exercise?
- Questions on gene therapy.
- Questions on the ethics of foetal transplantation.
- Questions on biochemistry and human biology.

Modern languages

Prepare for comprehension and translations, and also to answer questions on a text given immediately prior to the interview. Also be prepared to have a short conversation in the pre-studied language that you have chosen to pursue at university.

- Questions which focus on the use of language in original texts.
- Describe aspects of this poem which you find interesting.
- Interpret this poem, commenting on the tone and the context.
- Why do you want to study this language and not another?
- Why is it important to study literature?
- What is the difference between literature and philosophy?
- Questions on cultural and historical context and genre in European literature.

- How important is analysis of narrative in the study of literature?
- How important is knowledge of the biography of the author in the study of their literature?
- What is language?

Natural sciences

- What is an elastic collision?
- What happens when two particles collide – one moving and one stationary?
- What is friction?
- Questions on carboxylic acids.
- What is kinetic energy? How does it relate to heat?

Oriental studies

- What do you know about the Chinese language and its structure?
- What are the differences between English and any Oriental language with which you are familiar?
- Does language have an effect on identity?
- Compare and contrast any ambiguities in the following sentences. 'Only suitable magazines are sold here.' 'Many species inhabit a small space.' 'He is looking for the man who crashed his car.'
- Comment on the following sentences. 'He did wrong.' 'He was wrong.' 'He was about to do wrong.'

Philosophy

- What is philosophy?
- Would you agree that if p is true and s believes p, then s knows p?
- Was the question you have just answered about knowing or about the meaning of the word 'know'?
- Comment on these statements/questions. 'I could be dreaming that I am in this interview./I do not know whether I am dreaming or not, therefore I do not know whether I am in this interview or not.' 'A machine has free will.' 'When I see red, could I be seeing what you see when you see green?'
- Is it a matter of fact or logic that time travels in one direction only?
- Is our faith in scientific method itself based on scientific method? If so, does it matter?
- I can change my hairstyle and still be me. I can change my political opinions and still be me. I can have a sex change and still be me. What is it then that makes me be me?
- Can it ever be morally excusable to kill someone?

Physics

Be prepared to answer any questions relating to the A level syllabus including the following.

- Questions on applied mathematics.
- Questions on mathematical derivations.
- How does glass transmit light?
- How does depressing a piano key make a sound?
- How does the voltage on a capacitor vary if the dielectric gas is ionised?
- How has physics influenced political thinking during the past century?

Politics

- Can you define 'government'? Why do we need governments?
- Can you differentiate between power and authority?
- What makes power legitimate?
- What would be the result of a 'state of nature'?
- How can you distinguish between a society, a state, and an economy?
- Will Old Labour ever be revived? If so, under what circumstances?
- What would you say to someone who claims that women already have equal opportunities?
- What would you do tomorrow if you were the leader of the former Soviet Union?
- How does a democracy work?
- What elements constitute the ideologies of the extreme right?
- What do you think of discrimination in favour of female parliamentarians?
- How would you improve the comprehensive system of education?
- Does the UN still have a meaningful role in world affairs?
- Is further EU enlargement sustainable?
- How important is national identity?
- Should medics pay more for their degrees?

Psychology

- Is neuropsychology an exact science? If not, is it useful?
- Questions on the experimental elucidation of the mechanisms underlying behaviour.
- Give some examples of why an understanding of chemistry might be important in psychology.
- A new treatment is tested on a group of depressives, who are markedly better in six weeks. Does this show that the treatment was effective?
- There are records of violent crimes that exactly mimic scenes of violence on television. Does this indicate that television causes real violence?

- How would you establish the quietest sound that you can hear as opposed to the quietest sound that you think you can hear?
- Why might one be able to remember items at the beginning and end of an aurally presented list better than items in the middle?
- Could a computer ever feel emotion?
- Is it ethically justifiable to kill animals for the purpose of research?
- What is emotional intelligence?

Sociology

- What is the value of the study of social anthropology?
- Do people need tabloids?
- How would you define terrorism?
- Do you believe in selective education? Are we participating in selective education here?
- Is it possible to pose a sociological problem without sociological bias?
- Does prison work?
- Are MPs only in it for the power?
- How has the study of race and racism changed over the past 20 years?

(See also questions on politics and psychology.)

Theology

- Does moral rectitude reside in the agent, the act, or its consequences?
- What, if anything, is wrong with voluntary euthanasia?
- What is the best reason that you can think of for believing in the existence of God? Do you think that this course could conceivably be persuasive on the issue?
- What relevance does theology have for art history?
- What relevance does archaeology have for theology?
- Can you comment on the portrayal of Jesus in John versus the other gospels?

Veterinary medicine

- Has your work experience influenced your future career aspirations?
- Can you discuss an aspect of animal physiology which has struck you as contrasting with what you know of human physiology?
- Would our knowledge of BSE have been of value in controlling foot and mouth disease?
- Tell me about the biochemistry of DNA.
- What animal did this skull belong to?

(See also questions on biological sciences and chemistry.)

Any questions?

At the end of the interview you may be asked if you have any questions to ask the interviewer(s). It is always a good idea to have a few questions up your sleeve. One or two is a good number; more than three questions is usually too many. Write them down on a notepad and bring it with you. You will appear professional and keen. You may be able to bring up one of your favourite topics that was not discussed during the main part of the interview.

If, after all your research, you still have questions about your course or college, this is the time to ask. If there was a topic covered during the interview that you didn't understand, you could enquire about where you can read more about it, or get further clarification from the interviewers themselves.

Presentation skills: making an impression without words

It is widely agreed amongst psychologists today that we make powerful impressions on other people simply through our physical appearance and body language. In fact some say that body language counts for over 90% of the first impression you make.

Going for interview is stressful and it would be strange if you were not a little nervous. But don't be afraid of your nerves. Use them to heighten your awareness of the way you move, speak, and engage with the interviewer(s). Below are some suggestions from John Meeske, a counselling psychologist at the MPW school.

- *'Always carry yourself well, especially when you first enter the room; hold your head high, stand up straight, and smile.*
- *Shake the interviewer's hand firmly (without hurting them) and make direct eye contact. We often look to see where to shake and forget to make eye contact at all.'*

Interviews will generally be conducted in the offices of a potential director of studies or tutor. These offices are often part-way between a living room and an office. You may be asked to settle on a comfortable armchair or sofa but end up sinking down into it. Alternatively you may be given a hard-backed chair to sit on and find yourself perching on the edge. Whichever it is, John Meeske advises:

- *'take a moment to accustom yourself to the chair; you don't want to feel uncomfortable for the whole interview*
- *lean forward slightly in the chair when you are spoken to; this shows that you are interested and engaged*

- *put down anything you are holding; this will prevent you from fiddling and will allow you to give your full attention to the interviewer.'*

If you are asked tricky questions or feel intimidated by your interviewer you may feel unsure about how to respond. But remember, the way you say something is often as important as what you say. Remain calm and leave a few seconds before you attempt an answer. Whilst you are thinking, look away from the interviewer briefly to steady your thoughts. When you are ready, bring your eyes back to the interviewer. John Meeske suggests that you:

- *'maintain good eye contact with anyone who addresses you, but be sure to use your gaze to invite others present to engage with your responses*
- *you can also use arm gestures to emphasise your points.'*

Even if the interview doesn't go as well as you wished, leave with poise. Hold your head high, smile, and remember to thank the interviewers for their time. Your first and last impressions will resonate strongly.

Dress relatively smartly to show that you are taking the process seriously and to mentally prepare yourself for this important event. If suits are not your style, however, don't feel you need to buy one. You must simply look presentable, clean and tidy. For boys: a smart pair of trousers or cords, clean shoes and a shirt are suitable. Girls: a smart skirt (no shorter than knee-length) or trousers and a modest top are suitable. Remember, your clothes should not speak more loudly than you.

The pooling system

The pooling system exists to ensure that all strong candidates get a good chance of being accepted by an Oxbridge college, but it means something slightly differently in Cambridge and Oxford.

At Cambridge, pooling happens after the first interview process. If you are a strong candidate, but there has been particularly high competition for places at your college, your interviewers may feel that they cannot offer you a place but that you deserve a place at Cambridge. They will then place you in the 'pool': a database that can be accessed by members of their faculty at different colleges. Academics at these other colleges, who may have spare places or weaker candidates, will then 'fish out' their choice of strong 'pooled' students and ask them to come for interviews at their college. These 'second round' or 'pooling' interviews take place at the college of the academic who selects you some time in the second part of December and a few weeks after the first round of interviews. If you are 'pooled' you still stand a chance of being accepted. Around 3,000 offers per year are made by preference colleges, 600–700 offers are made through the pool.

At Oxford, 'pooling' happens at the same time as the first round interviews. This is the reason Oxford keeps applicants for several days during the interview process. You may be seen by other members of the faculty at different colleges during your stay. If you are a particularly strong candidate, academics at several colleges might ask you to interview, even if they are not at the college of your first choice and even if the academics at your preferred college already know they want to offer you a place. Whereas at Cambridge, being asked to a second round of interviews usually means you have not secured a place at your preferred college, at Oxford more interviews may mean the opposite. This also means that, whereas in Cambridge you will be sent home swiftly and then called up later, at Oxford prospective students may be kept hanging around for several days at a time whilst the academics battle things out between themselves.

Interview stories from previous applicants

Adam, Economics, Cambridge

Two weeks before my interview I was sent an interview pack from Cambridge, which contained an article that I read in advance of the interview, a few maps of the college and of Cambridge, some information about the interviews, and a food voucher for the food hall.

My interview was at midday. I could have stayed over the night before but I live close so I didn't. There were no designated student helpers and I got a bit lost in the college (it is very large) so I asked some people for help and directions. I would recommend going to the porter's lodge if you get very lost and they will direct you.

My first interview was the specialist interview for economics. I was interviewed by two fellows, who invited me to sit down on a couch as I entered the room where the interview took place. One interviewer sat directly in front of me and the other sat at a desk looking to the side. The interviewer who sat in front of me was the main interviewer, as the other interviewer hardly ever intervened and just took notes. The interview started with the principal interviewer asking me about what current events in the news had interested me most. I responded by talking about Northern Rock. She asked me why I was interested in what was happening at the time with Northern Rock. I told her that it stemmed from my great interest in economics and related it to out-of-class reading I had done on banking systems. The interview continued in that same tone and style. It was a very sober, tense environment. The interview was very formal and no time was lost on discussions that did not relate to economics.

I was sent an article a couple of weeks prior to the interview and I was asked a few questions on it. The answers basically related back to my A level knowledge of the subject. Then I was given a paragraph on economics and was told to comment on it. The comment could be anything I wanted to say or thought about the paragraph. It had some errors, that were not grammatical; it rested on dubious theory such as 'if you raise taxes, people will spend more', whereas I have been taught that if you raise taxes people will spend less.

Then they asked me a mathematical problem. They gave me a whiteboard to solve it on. It was a geometric problem. The problem was that there were two pieces of carpet and you had to cover an entire room with those two pieces of carpet. The trick was you could only make one cut. This seemed to me to be impossible. I was told to do what I could and I talked through the logic of finding the solution to the problem. I was stopped after around 30 seconds. After the maths question, the interviewers asked me if I had any questions. I asked them about fiscal policy and we had a short discussion and then the interview came to an end.

My general interview was very relaxed. The admissions tutor asked me questions such as 'Why Cambridge?', 'Why this college?' and 'Tell me five words your friends would use to describe you'. I was also told to describe an object as if I was on the telephone with the admissions tutor and they could not see the object. After I described the object, he asked me why I thought he had asked that question. This laid-back style characterised the interview. It was quite an enjoyable experience. The interviewer's questions were either very general and expected or very diverse, unusual, and startling.

Melissa, Human Sciences, Oxford

I had two interviews which seemed to me more like discussions than any sort of interrogation. I had done a mock interview in order to prepare and I was pleased that I had, because its style had prepared me for the worst! When I arrived, the undergraduates at the college were incredibly helpful, as they were able to give me an insight into what my interviewers were like, and they told me what little they could remember of their own interviews too.

The first interview lasted around 30 minutes and took place in an office just big enough for the two of us. The interviewer started by telling me about himself and some recent research he had been doing – I was so shocked by this because I had expected everything to be about me! It calmed me down, though, because it was like an ordinary conversation. He then started to ask me why I had chosen this subject over others that might have seemed more obvious for someone with my A levels. We then moved on to some technical questions. For one I had to comment on a graph showing the typical age when people die in certain countries. As I had not looked at this beforehand I had to think on my feet.

My interviewer had looked at the work I had sent in, and asked me to look at how one of the essays related to the subject I was applying for. He let me talk on about this for what seemed like ages and asked me lots of things about it. He seemed interested but I couldn't really tell what he thought of me.

In the second interview, I felt far more challenged but not in a confrontational way. When I was asked a question and gave an answer the interviewer would ask me yet another question on my answer. A common question she asked was 'Why?'. It was a very exciting interview and she seemed genuinely interested in what I had to say. Although I think I tackled a lot of it well on my own, she often prompted me to get me thinking along the right lines.

Both the interviewers were very friendly and seemed to be keen to find my strengths rather than my weaknesses. On the whole, I suppose, I actually enjoyed the experience!

Grace, History, Oxford

When I arrived at Oxford for the interview I was terribly nervous. I was taken through to a small study where two female professors were sitting. As soon as I walked in, I could sense that the atmosphere was much more relaxed than I had imagined it would be. The initial questions they asked me were drawn from points I had made in my Personal Statement, many of them about the Holy Grail. This immediately made me feel more relaxed, as I was confident about being able to support what I had written in my Personal Statement.

It was clear to me that they were not trying to trick me by asking questions about historical periods I hadn't covered. They were far more interested in the periods I had covered and were trying to engage me in debate by contradicting a number of the arguments I put forward.

After around 20 minutes, the questions became focused on an essay I had submitted prior to the interview. The questions were designed to make me look at alternative arguments to those I had used in my essay, and they made me question whether my arguments were right. However, when one of the interviewers asked me a question that seemed to have numerous correct answers, I realised that they were more interested in my ability to analyse different points of view.

I enjoyed my interview but I was not offered a place.

Imogen, French and Italian, Oxford

I was called for an interview about 10 days before the provisional date, but the letter did nothing except confirm that I had been called. There were no times or details given. Upon arrival at Oxford, the night before the interviews began, I learnt that the next day I had a language test and an Italian interview, and a French interview the following day.

Oxford prefers not to allow candidates to make their own way to interviews, in case they get lost, so each college has a general waiting room and a group of current undergraduate helpers to accompany everyone. On the morning of the test, all the modern linguists gathered in the waiting room, and we were shown to classrooms where we had to take a grammar test in each of the languages we were applying for, except those we were intending to study from scratch. I sat tests in French and Italian, lasting an hour in total, and consisting of translation and multiple choice questions.

My Italian interview took place at Balliol (I applied to St Anne's), because there is no Italian fellow at St Anne's. A student helper took me to Balliol, and I was given an Italian poem to look at. This was discussed in my interview and I was then asked to talk about subjects I had brought up in my Personal Statement. We then discussed various books I had read and, surprisingly, did not speak any Italian.

I had one interviewer for the first Italian interview. This was a very strange interview. I was given an Italian poem (*Canzonetta sulle sirene catodiche* by Magrelli) to read and make notes on before I was called in.

- I had to describe aspects of the poem which I found interesting.
- I was then asked to summarise my Personal Statement as he hadn't seen it before.
- Then he asked me why I thought that Primo Levi was a good writer, told me that his book was originally rejected by Natalia Ginzburg, and asked what I felt about that.
- The conversation then moved on to Dante, and he wanted to know how I had approached my study of *L'Inferno*, and which of the *canti* I had enjoyed.
- I was then given the opportunity to ask him a question.

The second part of the interview consisted of a discussion of a poem and I had two interviewers. When I met the interviewers they gave me a poem to read in English.

- Again, the poem was discussed in depth, but this time I was pushed to interpret bits which were harder to understand, rather than just comment on bits I liked.
- The interviewer then picked up on the Primo Levi in my Personal Statement, and asked me what I thought of the quote 'After Auschwitz, no more poetry', with reference to the philosophy I studied at school.

- There was a brief conversation in Italian, focusing on current affairs and places I had visited in Italy.
- Again I was allowed to ask a question.

The next morning I had a French interview at St Anne's. Again I was given a passage to read, again in English, which was discussed with one of the interviewers.

There was a conversation in French with a second interviewer, which covered some literature and my reasons for studying French. Lastly, the third interviewer asked some slightly more in-depth questions about the importance of literature, and the relationship between literature and phi-losophy (I had made some references to philosophy in my Personal Statement).

I had three interviewers for my first French interview. I was given another passage in English; it was an extract from the works of Edgar Allan Poe.

- I was asked questions about the tone of the passage, what situation I thought the extract was taken from, and how I felt the episode would conclude.
- Then we had a conversation in French about why I wanted to study French as opposed to any other language, what I felt the themes were in the film *Jules et Jim* by Francois Truffaut (the essay I sent up was based on this film), and what I felt the film said about the difference between the French and the Germans during the war.
- I was asked a series of questions, including: Why is it important to study literature? What is the difference between literature and phi-losophy? What French book had I recently read that I enjoyed? I talked about *La Princesse de Cleves*.

My second interview for French had two interviewers. This time I was given a poem to read in French. There was a note at the top saying that I should try to understand the poem, but not to worry if I didn't know all the vocabulary, because I would be asked which bits of the poem I found most interesting and was not expected to understand it all.

- However, I was then fired a series of questions on every verse of the poem, and interrupted during every answer to be further questioned on why I thought that, where I was getting my informa-tion from, and could I give more examples to back up my point. Luckily, I had been placed in a library to read through the passage, and so had looked up all the unfamiliar vocabulary. The moral of the story – don't believe the kindly worded instructions!
- One of the interviewers then said he was intrigued as to my interest in Ronsard, and we discussed where the major Petrarchan influences were in the poetry.

 ● Then followed a French conversation where I had to talk about my work placement in Le Touquet, and what I thought the differences were between French and British holidaymakers.

I had been told that I would be allowed to leave Oxford at 10am the following morning, but that some candidates would be required to stay until later the next day to attend interviews at other colleges.

Madeleine, Modern and Medieval Languages, Cambridge

Shortly after I had sent off my UCAS form, Cambridge contacted me by letter to give me details of the written work they required, which in my case was two essays; one for Latin and one for Italian. I wrote an essay in English for the Latin requirement, and a short essay based on an A level topic in Italian. These essays were due early in November.

I was then called to interview, again by letter, which arrived roughly halfway through November, and was told all the details and times of the tests and interviews I would be expected to sit, which all took place on one day in the first half of December.

I stayed in college the night before my interviews, due to an early start the next day, which I would highly recommend as it gives one the opportunity to get used to the surroundings, talk to current students, and it means that it isn't a great rush in the morning before the interview.

I had to sit a test first, and as a language applicant I had to choose one of my languages in which to answer. In my case, it had to be Italian, but as it turned out, very little of the test was actually in the foreign language. There was a passage to be read, in English, which I had to summarise in a foreign language (Italian), and then I had to answer a very broad essay question in English. The test lasted an hour.

My first interview was a couple of hours later, so I took the opportunity to have lunch with some friends who were also applying to other colleges, whilst making sure I left myself plenty of time to get to the interview, which was for the Latin side of my application. I was given some Latin poetry to read, try to understand, and analyse, and this was then discussed in the interview. I was also questioned about the essay I had sent up, and was given some general questions about why I had applied for the course and what my gap year plans were. In this particular interview, there were two interviewers.

Following this was my Italian interview, which was conducted by one person only. Again, I was given a passage to try to understand and talk about, and then we discussed the literature that I was studying for my A2. Finally, she asked me a couple of questions in Italian to test my standard of speaking, focusing on where I had visited in Italy.

After this, I was free to leave, with nothing else to do but wait for the result. At Cambridge the results are all given out on one day, shortly after Christmas, and this date is stated in advance. There will be one of three possible results given on this day, either an acceptance, a rejection, or the news that you have been placed in the 'winter pool', which means that there is a possibility that another college will accept you, based on the strength of your UCAS form. Acceptance or rejection from this pool can be held until as late as the end of January, during which time there is the possibility of being called for further interviewing.

John, Modern and Medieval Languages (Latin), Cambridge

I was given a 20-line passage of Ovid's *Metamorphoses*, about half an hour before the start of the interview, and left in the library to look at it. I was then taken to the interview room. I was addressed first by the general admissions tutor for modern and medieval languages, who asked me what had brought me to my choice of languages (Latin and Italian), and which aspects of the course at Cambridge appealed. She then asked me lots of questions about the gap year I intended to take, how I thought it would be beneficial to me, and how I planned to keep my study skills alive whilst I was away.

The rest of the interview was taken by the Latin lecturer, who started by asking me some grammatical questions about the passage I had looked at. I had to translate bits of it, and then identify some literary techniques used. We then talked about the passage in general, about the themes, and general storyline.

The interviewer then brought up the essay I had sent, which was an analysis of Book I of Virgil's *Aeneid*. He questioned me quite intensely on one comment I had made, until I couldn't defend myself any longer.

We discussed my Personal Statement, in particular the references I had made to Linear B, an ancient Mycenaean language, and I was asked what reading I had done to develop this unusual interest. Lastly, he asked me to imagine that I was talking to someone who had never studied classics before, and to recommend them one book to read and explain my choice.

10| Getting the letter
Offer or rejection and how to cope

Once you have had your interview, you may have to wait several weeks before you hear the result. If you applied to Oxford you may hear before Christmas, but you will normally hear from Cambridge in early January. A firm or unconditional offer will be made only if you already have your A level grades, for example, if you have taken a gap year. This means you definitely have a place.

If the college wants to accept you, you will normally get a conditional offer. This is an offer on the condition that you meet the required grades in your A levels. Your place, therefore, will only be confirmed on results day in August. The offer may be 'general', for example, A*AA, or 'specific', where the college asks for an A* in a particular subject. Most colleges make a standard offer of A*AA at Cambridge and AAA at Oxford. Some will stipulate that you need to get 90% in certain A level modules. If, on results day, your grades are what you needed to obtain to win your place, there is no need to make contact with your college. Your grades have already been communicated to the university and your place will be confirmed via letter and email.

If you are unsuccessful, you will receive a rejection letter in the post between December and mid-January. If this is the case for you, do not despair. Remember that there is incredibly high competition to get a place at Oxbridge. Although for many subjects one in five students interviewed are accepted, for other subjects 10 students are interviewed for one place. More than 5,000 of the unsuccessful applicants per year will have been predicted three As at A level, and are clearly intelligent and successful students.

If you are rejected, despite having gained As and A*s at A level, and you want to know why, ring the admissions tutor at your chosen college and ask for feedback. If your grades are good and you are really set on claiming a place at Oxbridge, think about why you did not succeed the first time and try again. Neither Cambridge nor Oxford looks badly on students who apply twice. You may have been too young the first time or too focused on school exams to dedicate enough time to the application process. Alternatively, you may not have made an appropriate subject choice and were not passionate enough about your field. If once was enough, however, focus on your other university choices and draw on your Oxbridge experiences to help you in your preparation for future interviews.

If you did not get the grades required by Oxbridge (for example you got an AAB rather than A*AA), your conditional offer will be withdrawn. You may wish to contact the admissions tutor at your college at this point, but you should be prepared for the fact that it is unlikely you will get a second chance. Oxford and Cambridge do not look kindly on retake students, unless of course there is a real and significant reason why you did not fulfil your potential in the exams (for example, illness or a bereavement in the family).

UCAS has recently introduced an 'Adjustment' system whereby students who get above their predicted grades can go back to universities who rejected them and try for a place again. However, it is unlikely that this system will apply to Oxford and Cambridge since they are always extremely oversubscribed. What you could do if your exam results exceed your expectations is to reapply the following year with your excellent grades, and try for a place that way.

Remember, if you are a motivated and focused student, then you will excel at whatever university you go to, and if you love your subject, then your interest will flourish wherever you are.

A word on stress

The whole process of applying to Oxford and Cambridge is very stressful and you need to be prepared for this. Taking A levels is intense and requires incredible stamina and concentration; you are not only competing against your peers, but your strength of character is tried. With your university application riding on the need for particularly good grades, you are more likely to put even more pressure on yourself than other students would. Then there is the UCAS form to complete, the word-perfect Personal Statement that has to be checked and checked again, and the experience of having to defend your ideas against academics who may seem like intellectual giants at interview. There is also the fear of rejection.

However, don't let this put you off. If you learn to compete against yourself, and to love the process of studying, and if you have a real fascination for the subject you wish to pursue, you will be able to deal with the competition at Oxbridge. If you don't get a place, you will have found a subject that you really enjoy and this will be an immense advantage, whichever university you go to.

Of course, taking regular breaks from study and discussing your fears with friends can be helpful, and at university students spend a lot of time comparing their workload with their peers and commiserating with each other. A good moan can often do wonders. Taking regular exercise, getting enough sleep, and keeping a circle of trusted friends around you can be very important when coping with stress. You should also remember that, if you are offered a place, the admissions tutors clearly believe you can cope, so you should believe it too! Have faith in yourself. Alternatively, if you don't get an offer, remember, there are many other universities that have world-renowned research departments, and that may offer you a healthier work–life balance!

Appendix 1: timetables

The year before you apply

March

- Request an undergraduate prospectus from the admissions office and the alternative prospectus from the student unions of Cambridge or Oxford.
- Book a place at an open day.
- Research other universities to which you are considering applying.

April

- Write the first draft of your Personal Statement.
- Go on an open day.

June

- Sit your AS levels.

Summer holidays

- Ask friends and family to read your Personal Statement and make revisions.
- Work experience.

The year in which you apply

September

- Finalise your Personal Statement with your teachers.
- Visit the UCAS website (www.ucas.com) and register.
- Fill in the UCAS form (UCAS applications may be submitted from 1 September).
- Register and book a place to sit the LNAT (if you want to study law at Oxford).
- Register for the BMAT exam if you are applying for medicine (at Oxford or Cambridge) or veterinary medicine (Cambridge only).

October

- The deadline for UCAS receiving your application form, whether for Oxford or Cambridge, is 15 October.
- If applying to Cambridge, fill in the separate Cambridge Supplementary Application Questionnaire. This will be emailed to you and must be completed by 31 October.

Late October

- Receive acknowledgement letter from your chosen college.
- Sit the HAT (for history applicants to Oxford).
- Sit the physics and maths for physics aptitude test (for physics or physics and philosophy applicants to Oxford).
- Sit the ELAT (for applicants to English at Oxford).
- Sit the Maths Aptitude Test (for applicants for maths or computer science at Oxford).

November

- Sit the BMAT exam in the first week of November if you are applying for medicine (at Oxford or Cambridge) or veterinary science (Cambridge only).
- Deadline for sitting LNAT (for people who want to study law at Oxford) is at the beginning of November.
- Receive letter inviting you to interview from Oxford or Cambridge and explaining if and when to submit written work. Alternatively you may receive a letter rejecting you at this point.
- Submit written work with the special form – see faculty website for details. (Work should be sent directly to the college unless you have made an 'open application', in which case send it directly to the faculty. The work should be marked by your school).

December

- If invited, attend interviews in the first three weeks of December (see precise interview dates for your subject in the prospectus).
- You may have to sit some tests at interview.
- At Cambridge you may have to sit the TSA.
- Before 25 December – hear the outcome of your application from Oxford.

January

- Beginning of January – applicants who have been placed in the 'winter pool' are notified (Cambridge only). This may or may not entail going to Cambridge for another set of interviews.

- Middle of January – hear outcome of your application from Cambridge.

June

- Sit A levels.
- After A levels sit STEP paper or AEA (maths only).

August

- Mid-August – results day.
- If you have made your grades your place will be confirmed by the university.
- If you have not made your grades, contact the admissions tutor for your college.
- You may be sent a letter of rejection at this point.

Appendix 2: glossary

Adjustment. When the A level exam results come out in August, students who do not make their offers or, alternatively, students who get much better grades than predicted, can enter a competition for universities that have spare places.

Admissions tutor. The tutor especially assigned the role of selecting candidates.

Alumni. People who once went to the college but who have now graduated.

Collections. Exams sat at the beginning of each term at Oxford in the colleges.

Collegiate system. This term describes the fact that both Oxford and Cambridge Universities are divided into about 30 separate colleges, where students live and where their social lives are based.

Deferred entry. This means you would like to take a gap year (i.e. defer your entry for a year). You apply this year but will accept a place in two years' time.

Deselected. Some candidates will not have made it to the interview; they are 'deselected' before the interview and will receive a letter of rejection.

DOS. Director of studies at Cambridge University. Your DOS is an academic member of staff from your subject faculty, who is also a fellow of your college. He or she is responsible for your academic development and will meet you at the beginning and end of each term to check on your progress and will probably be your interviewer. The DOS at Cambridge is the equivalent to a tutor at Oxford.

Exhibitions. A scholarship you can win in recognition of outstanding work at Oxford.

Faculty. The department building dedicated to one particular subject area, for example, the Faculty of Architecture.

Fellow. A fellow is an academic member of a college. Each academic in every faculty is also assigned a college; this is where their office space is located. Some more senior fellows are given responsibility for the academic achievement of the students at their college and act as the DOS (at Cambridge) or tutor (at Oxford) of a number of undergraduates.

Fresher. First year undergraduate student.

Go up. Traditionally, instead of simply saying 'go to university' for Oxford and Cambridge the term used is to 'go up' to university.

Open application. A way of applying to either Oxford or Cambridge without specifying a college.

Oxbridge. The collective term for Oxford and Cambridge.

Permanent private halls. These are like mini-colleges in Oxford; two of them – St Benet's Hall (men only) and Regent's Park College (men and women) – are for students studying any subject, but the remaining five are mainly for people who are training to be in the ministry.

Pool. The pool is the place where applicants who are rejected by their first-choice college are held until another college selects them for an interview. The other college may do this for a variety of reasons, such as if they have not got enough good applicants and want to find some better ones, or if they want to check that their weakest chosen student is better than another college's rejected student – a sort of moderation process.

Porter's lodge. Your first port of call at an Oxford or Cambridge college. This is where post gets delivered and where, if you get lost, they will be able to direct you – a bit like reception.

Porters. The porters are the men and women who act like wardens of the lodge.

Read. Instead of 'studying' a subject, the verb used is to 'read' a subject.

Subfusc. The black gown, black trousers/skirt and white shirts Oxford students must wear to take exams.

Summon. Another way to say 'to be called' for interview.

Supervision. A class held on a one-to-one basis or in a small group with your tutor (in Cambridge).

Tripos. Word used to describe how Cambridge degree courses are divided into blocks of one or two years, called Part I and Part II.

Tutor. At Oxford University your tutor is an academic member of staff from your subject faculty, who is also a fellow of your college. He or she is responsible for your academic development and will meet you on a regular basis to check on your progress, and will probably be your interviewer. The DOS at Cambridge is the equivalent to a tutor at Oxford.

Tutorial. A class held on a one-to-one basis or in a small group with your tutor (at Oxford).

Appendix 3: the UCAS form

1. Go to www.ucas.com/students/apply to register in the September of your A2 year. In order to do this you will need an email address. If you haven't got one go to yahoo.com or hotmail.com and get a free one. When you register on the UCAS website, you will be sent an application number, user name, and password, which you will need every time you log on to UCAS.
2. The entire application is done online and although it may seem complex and time-consuming, you can complete it in stages and come back to it. There are 'help' sections all the way through the form in case you get stuck.
3. Fill in the 'Personal details' section, which includes your name, address, and date of birth.
4. Fill in the 'Student support' section, which is where you have to select your fee code. If you are a British national your local authority will be your fee payer.
5. Next is an 'Additional information' section in which you can list the activities you have done in preparation for further education. These activities specifically refer to attending summer schools in preparation for university run by either the universities themselves or trusts such as the Sutton Trust. See www.suttontrust.com or contact UCAS for more information (www.ucas.com/about_us/contact_us).
6. The fifth section is where you enter your 'University choices'. You can apply to either Oxford or Cambridge. Choose the correct university code from the drop-down menu (CAM C05 for Cambridge and OXF 033 for Oxford). You also need to write what UCAS calls the 'campus code', which is the college code. A drop-down list will appear again. You will also need to choose the subject and select which year of entry you are applying for.
7. The next section asks you for details of your education. You need to write down every GCSE and A level (or equivalent qualification) you have taken and what grade you got under the heading of the school in which you took them. If you are applying post-A level you need to write down all of your module grades.
8. The next section is 'Employment'. This does not ask you about work experience, but about paid employment. It is worth writing down even the most insignificant jobs you have done – washing dishes at the local restaurant, for example – since admissions tutors will value the commitment and maturity you will have shown when holding down a job.

9. Next is the 'Personal Statement'. This is your chance to show the admissions tutors how you write and how informed you are about your subject. You should write this in a Word document, spell check it and read it through carefully, and when it is ready, copy and paste it into the UCAS form. The Personal Statement is discussed in more detail in Chapter 7.

10. Finally, send the form off in the first week of October to be completed by your teachers. In order to do this, you have to pay £19 (or £9 if you are applying to just one university) to UCAS to process your information. This must be paid by credit card (your school may have a policy of paying this for you so you need to check before you part with any money). Your teacher will then be able to open it on the teachers' part of the UCAS site. They will read it to check everything is correct and will then write their reference and predicted grades. Your teacher may need some time to write the reference, so do make sure you have your part done well in advance.

11. Your teachers then need to send your UCAS form to Oxford and Cambridge by 15 October. This will arrive at the universities immediately.

Appendix 4: maps

Oxford map

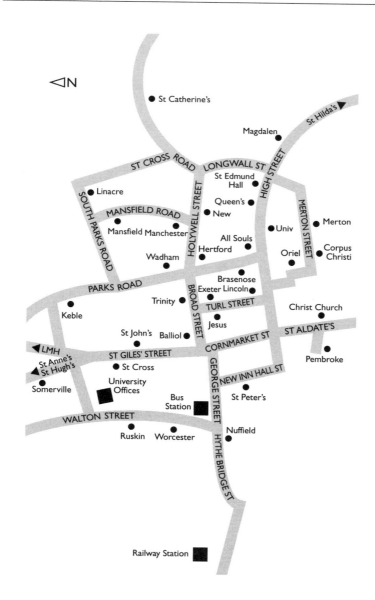

Cambridge map

Postscript

If you have followed the advice in this book then you will have certainly given Oxford or Cambridge your best shot. Good luck, and remember that you will be successful at whichever university you attend.

MPW (London)

90–92 Queen's Gate

London

SW7 5AB

Tel: 020 7835 1355

Fax: 020 7259 2705

Email: enquiries@mpw.co.uk